C0-DUO-147

Thrive and Prosper

Insider Strategies and Inspiring Stories For Entrepreneurs That Help Create Success In Your Business, Relationships, and Life

Mary Silver MSW

Get Your Bonus Gifts & Free Resources Here

Scan or Click Here To Download Your Bonus Gifts & Free Resources!
qrco.de/bcrTuK

To say thank you for purchasing Thrive and Prosper, we'd love to offer you bonus gifts and free resources by scanning the picture above!

Copyright And Terms of Use

Terms of Use:

You are given a non-transferable, personal use license to this book. There are no resale rights or private label rights granted when purchasing this book. In other words, it's for your own personal use only.

Copyright © 2022 by Mary Silver MSW – Baillee Enterprises LLC.

All rights reserved. No part of this publication may be reproduced, distributed or transmitted in any form or by any means including, photocopying, recording, or other electronic or mechanical methods without the prior written permission of the publisher, except in the case of brief quotations embodied in critical reviews and certain **other non-commercial uses permitted by copyright law.**

Publisher: Silver Lining Publishing LLC

Legal Disclaimer

By reading this book, you assume all risk associated with using the advice given, with a full understanding that you, solely, are responsible for anything that may occur as a result of putting this information into action in any way, and regardless of your interpretation of the advice.

You further agree that the author and the co-authors, any company owned by her or them, cannot be held responsible in any way for the success or failure of your business, relationships, or life as a result of the information presented in this book. It is your responsibility to conduct your own due diligence regarding the safe and successful operation of your business, relationships, and life if you intend to apply any of our information and any way to your business operations, relationships, and life.

This book is not intended as a substitute for the medical advice of physicians. The reader should consult a physician in matters relating to his/her health and particularly with respect to any symptoms that may require diagnosis or medical attention.

Contents

Welcome To Thrive and Prosper!

Scan or click on the above QR code to claim your bonus gifts and free resources from the featured authors! qrco. de/bcrTuK

Thrive and Prosper - Insider Strategies and Inspiring Stories For Entrepreneurs That Help Create Success In Your Business, Relationships, and Life is a book that came together due to the rising chaos that is going on throughout the entire world. First, there is a world-wide pandemic that we are all coming out of. Due to mandatory stay at home orders imposed because of the pandemic, many people lost their homes, businesses, relationships, and more. We have cultural inclusion awareness issues surfacing that need to be addressed. It has caused division, riots, and hate crimes, making many people feel uneasy throughout the world. Also, there is a war between Russian and Ukraine going on that has the world on edge, while driving gas and oil prices through the roof. It is truly heart-wrenching. Hopefully, these issues will be resolved soon. In the meantime, the experts showcased throughout this book are giving you their very best stuff to equip you with more ways to create success in your business, relationships, and life.

Welcome To Thrive and Prosper!

As a mentor to upcoming leaders, online coaches, and visionaries, I keep hearing stories about how many of you were feeling anxious about your future and the state of your business. People were reporting having an increase in tension in their relationships and life in general. While I was meditating, I was asking myself, "What can I do to help more people? What can I do that can help in a better way?" That is how the idea of this book was formed.

I knew that I couldn't do it on my own. So, I enlisted 15 authors that specialize in the areas of business, relationships, and life for online entrepreneurs, coaches, and visionaries. I knew with their input and expertise; we could write a powerful book that would help as many people as we could. Together, we can create a mass awareness of the strategies and inspirational stories that have helped them during times of crisis, and their clients. Our hope is to create healing and help transform the stress and tension that so many people are feeling right now. When healing occurs in these areas, you can focus on your heart's true desire and create the success you know you were born for!

Now let's get on with it, shall we?

Love and hugs,
Mary

Mary Silver MSW - International Best-Selling Author, Success, & Book Mentor to Upcoming Leaders, Coaches, & Visionaries, helps get your message out in powerful ways through the power of your authority positioning book! By publishing a book focused on your soul work, you are seen as the expert. You attract your soulmate clients into your aligned profit paths, and create an online dynasty with ease. This gives you the financial freedom, time freedom, the ability to serve more at every level, while only doing the work you came here to do! To learn more about Mary's services, go to https://www.marybaileysilver.com/

Chapter 1

Mary Silver MSW ~ International Best-Selling Author & Success Coach

Creating Profit Paths For Your Purpose Work Through The Power Of Your Book

Every online coach and visionary wants to make an impact. You want to make the world a better place with the transformational work that you do. Most often, I hear you want to create a ripple effect of healing so that more people live in prosperity and abundance. I couldn't agree more!

After spending 20 years helping people create a better life for themselves, this is exactly how I feel. Without a doubt, I can say, the most powerful thing you can do the manifest your desires and see the abundance of good in the world is to get your message out to millions, to impact millions with your words!

So many times, I've seen new online coaches and visionaries get sucked down the path of the newest and latest ways to make your business successful. This usually leads to burnout and overwhelm. You simply can't do it all.

· · ·

1

The problem here is these strategies may or may not align with you and your purpose work. As an example, let's talk about social media. Most online entrepreneurs will tell you they don't like that part of marketing their business. They say they feel like they're wasting time, like they're a fraud, or lost in a sea of others that do exactly what they do. Yet, time and time again, they purchase a program, product, or app to help them master the newest and greatest platform.

The sad news is, most people won't make any sales from social media unless it's from paid ads. Why? It isn't aligned, and it's a skill that takes months, if not years, to profit from. Unless you have a large following of people who have worked with you, or who know someone who has had great results from working with you, it doesn't work! It takes a ton of time to be seen on social media, and then build trust. Let me ask you, how much time do you have?

Think about it. When was the last time you saw a relatively unknown online coach making bank off of social media when they were selling their service or coaching package? I can assure you, it's not often. I have participated and I'm part of many high-level mastermind programs, and I can tell you 98% of the members will admit that they don't sell well through social media channels unless they are paying for ads.

Now, before you get upset, I'm not bashing social media. It's a great *tool to assist* your business. It's *not an efficient strategy* to start with in order to create a profitable business, doing your purpose work, aligning with your soulmate clients, so you aren't chasing them down. Especially at the beginning of your career. It takes too long to get that kind of traction from social media. Sure, there is the one percent that have an instant hit, but that is not even close to the reality for most.

The sad news is most online coaches and visionaries will go out of business within the first two years of business. The last time I looked into that statistic was three months before writing this book. That number had reached 82% that will go out of business by the end of the second year in business. That is not great news.

The reason they go out of business? They are chasing, using strategies that don't align with their energy, taking course after course (and most of the time, not finishing those courses), wasting hours a day trying to gain traction on social media, jumping from strategy to strategy, which leaves them exhausted, broke, overwhelmed, confused, and out of alignment with their soul work.

I'm going to let you in on a secret. The best and fastest way to create profits in your business is to **become the authority!** Yes, that is the way to create your wildly successful business and online dynasty! The question is, how do you go about doing that?

Write
Your Author Authority
Acceleration Code Book!

What does that even mean? Let me break it down for you in 5 steps.

- Align with your purpose work
- Create a framework for your purpose work
- Write your authority producing book, showcasing your soul work
- Publishing your authority positioning book
- Sell your book and lead your soulmate clients into your aligned profit path

Looks pretty simple now, doesn't it!

Hands down, a book is the best and fastest way to creating on online dynasty through aligned profit paths. Before I go any further, let me explain what I mean when I say an online dynasty. It's your online store with a variety of products, programs, services, books, and any other way people can work with you. It's available online, anytime, anywhere, by anyone! Meaning, you don't have to be actively selling every minute of every day. Your dynasty is like a castle that people get to visit whenever they want. But how do they know where your dynasty is located? Hint, hint. It's through your book!

Another question I get is, what is an aligned profit path? An aligned profit path is the way you like to work, the way the FEELS most natural to you. It's the material, technique, or method you are teaching that comes from your soul or your purpose work. It's aligned with you. The profit path leads your soulmate clients into your business like magic. It magnetizes them because they feel drawn to you. When they are aware and resonate with you, they want to know how to work with you. When you have a path for them to find you (another hint: it's your book), you can easily sell to them because they already feel like they know, like, and trust you. It makes selling to them joyful and fun!

The power of your book is endless. You can write more than one. You can write on different topics, creating a new and different aligned profit path. You can unleash your creativity and start enjoying the work you need to do to create the financial freedom, time freedom, impact millions, create a ripple effect of transformation, and manifest all the things that you desire!

Writing your book gives you instant credibility as the expert on your topic. People will see you as someone who has deep knowledge or understanding of a skill set or modality. They will start to feel like they know you and are aligned with you. People will also see that you back yourself around your work. Which when it comes down to it, most online coaches and visionaries don't back themselves or their work.

Writing and publishing a book can be and is very confronting. Your subconscious mind chatters about how you aren't good enough to write a book on the subject. Or something along those lines. Not to mention the possibility of people leaving negative reviews or not liking your work. When you put yourself out there, you open yourself up to unwanted criticism. This activates the fear center in your brain. Your brain is designed to keep you safe. If you are in fear mode, your mind thinks you're in danger and will do anything in its power to keep you safe. This is why people self-sabotage!

Ouch! That hurts. That is why most people won't write a book around their purpose work. They allow their fear brain to rule and they stop themselves from getting to the other side, which is wild success. If you have any doubts, I'm here to change your mind, because I personally know the power of a book! So get over the negative conscious and subconscious chatter and write your authority making book!

When you have the credibility of being a published author on your topic, you will be seen as the expert and the authority on the subject. There's no way around it! People are always impressed by coaches and visionaries that write a book! You become the go-to expert on the subject! Raise your hand if you want that!

When you have authority and are seen as an expert, opportunities that you never had before show up. People will start reaching out to you so that they can work with you. They'll resonate with you and your style and will practically beg to work with you. Your calendar fills up on autopilot just because you had the guts to put your purpose work out to the masses, making it easy for your soulmate clients to find you! Your book will always be working for you to bring in new leads that are perfect clients for you!

You won't have to run around chasing people at networking events or on social media. You can do those things if they feel aligned, and it brings in cold hard cash. But if they don't, you're wasting your time and resources. With your book that showcases you and puts you in the spotlight, you won't have to push so hard to make things work just so you have income coming into your business. It happens as if by magic, and on autopilot.

With your author authority, you will be able to promote your work to other industry leaders and to the media. When you have the power of your authority positioning book behind you, the media and your peers take you more seriously. They see that you have put in the work and know what you're talking about. They'll want to do features and stories about you. They'll want to partner up with you because you've made it easy for them to see your value and the level of service you give up front.

It makes collaborations and joint venture partnerships so much easier to come by. You'll be asked to speak on summits or speak at events. The people you have always wanted to partner with will actually reach out to you! Again, no more chasing is necessary. Please understand, there is definitely a strategy around this, but it happens with joy and ease when it is done correctly!

Then something amazing happens. With your authority positioning book, you get to create all your programs, products, and services around your unique framework, making it simple to sell more. Why? Because it *is* unique and special. It's not like any other work out there. You are a leader, and even if your framework centers on a technique or concept you learned from someone else, nobody does it like you do. Period! End of story!

You'll never need to create something to sell just for the sake of making money. Your purpose work fuels your soul and without it, you know a part of you would die. All your ideas and creation get to come alive because you're aligned and motivated to create services of value and deep meaning to you. Imagine being inspired every day by your career because you get to do ONLY what you love to do. You manifest money through your business because you are aligned and spotlighting yourself as the expert in the area of your purpose work. Now doesn't that feel AMAZING!

When you understand how the power of your author authority acceleration code works with your book, the skies the limit. Here are the creations and manifestations you get to experience when you write your authority positioning book:

- A best-selling book
- Instant credibility
- Acknowledgement around your expertise
- Showcasing yourself as a leader and change maker who creates the transformation and ripple effect to impact millions
- A profit path that directs money into your business with ease and in a way that is aligned with your soul work
- Having multiple aligned profit paths that allow you to work with clients on all levels, making sure you aren't leaving money on the table
- An easier way to land speaking gigs, both online and offline.
- Be seen in the media
- Collaborate with the people you have admired for years
- And last but not least, manifest your online dynasty that generates as much money as you desire, working with your soulmate clients, while doing your purpose work, with ease and flexibility, so that you can have financial freedom, time freedom, authority, credibility, contribute more, and impact millions with your work!

As a leader who is ready to step up and own your authority, isn't it time you write your book?

If this sounds like something you want to explore, be sure to check out my Unleash Your Best Seller - 5 Steps to Best Seller gift that's available to download. Simply Scan or Click on the QR code Below! qrco.de/bcrTuK

Let's get you seen, heard, and paid as the authority in your field and create your lasting legacy now!

Scan or click on the above QR code to claim your bonus gifts and free resources from the featured authors! qrco.de/bcrTuK

Chapter 2

Rach Wilson

**How Addressing Your Relationship Stuff
Ignites Growth in Your Business!**

Your Business and Your Relationship ARE Connected... Fixing One,
Boosts The Other.

What you are going to read in this chapter is a rather unique way to approach troubleshooting what's causing your business drains and blocks, and is also a new way of boosting your business' attraction factor. I promise you, when you understand how it all fits together, you'll be like, "oh duh! Of course!"

The mistake most entrepreneurs make is to try to work on specific areas of their lives to make them better. They are focusing on their business when the business is struggling, or their health when their body and energy are struggling, or their relationship when it's feeling hard. While all of that is true and can totally make those issues better, what's been completely overlooked is that we are dynamic beings.

At the heart of every area of our lives is the exact same thing; *US*. When we are affected by something or struggling in one area, whether it be our business or our relationship when it's not working, it naturally impacts and flows into other areas. Why? Because part of us is consumed by it, bringing our energy down.

We are a full ecosystem within ourselves. We don't compartmentalize like we think!

Knowing all of that, and knowing that *YOU* are at the center of every area of your life, why aren't more people looking to the various other areas of their lives? Why aren't they looking outside of the challenged area to find the answer and solutions, in order to completely transform it all?

Well, this is why I'm here. We're going to explore specifically how your relationship state, patterns, skills and baggage directly impacts your business. And on the flip side, how your business behaviors, drivers, patterns, and baggage steal what could be an EPIC relationship out from under your nose.

Let me ask you some questions. The purpose of these is to help you see, in real time, what I mean by all of that. It's all nice to read something and go, "This makes sense", but it's something entirely different when you start to apply it! I highly recommend you grab a notebook and pen to write the answers to these questions. They might give you some really important insights!

- What issues are you currently having in your relationship? Notice the emotions you feel, and what's triggering you to feel them. Even if you don't have a relationship and you're currently ruminating on what you're missing out on, write about that.

EXAMPLES:

1. **Not getting enough quality time.** You are consistently working long hours to build the business so you can "both" reap the benefits of the freedom that comes with a successful one. You justify the long hours and focus by saying, "I'm

doing this for US", but it's constantly a bone of contention between you.

2. **Communication Issues.** These occur when one or both of you are not asking for what you want or need. Another way this shows up is, there are regular misunderstandings because your communication is not clear. Equally, emotions getting triggered beyond a reasonable level, making something that could be simple to resolve, into a much more complex and intensely draining event.

3. **Lack of passion and purpose.** Not having enough energy or time to spend getting your sexy on!

4. **People pleasing patterns.** This looks like all the things you do to avoid conflict and keep the other person happy, often sacrificing what you need or want to say in the process.

5. **Guilt** which then becomes a wall between you. You feel guilty because you are spending so much time on your business and not with your partner. Or you feel guilty because your business isn't as successful as you thought it would be by now, adding financial strain because you're not contributing as much as you feel you should be. Guilt can show up because you feel you should be able to "give back" to them for all of their sacrifice to support you in building your business, and still can't.

6. **Not feeling good enough.** You feel like you can't meet all of their needs (and/or vice versa), can't get it right and may never be able to meet their expectations (even if this is only *YOUR* perceived expectations).

- Whatever you wrote above, ask yourself if you are having similar issues in your business, particularly with your clients. Try it on. It may not look exactly the same, but often it's there.
- What other issues are happening in your business?

EXAMPLES:

1. **Overwhelm** - Overwhelm from trying to do everything and get it right. Things such as the right marketing strategy, then implementing it, and getting it to work asap!
2. **Scarcity or lack mindsets and energy** - Worried about not making enough money and having that drive your decisions and action. This often results in taking a LOT of action with limited or inconsistent results.
3. **Attracting clients who aren't committing fully** - They want you to work at times you hadn't planned on, negotiating to pay less, or who are just plain hard work. If you find yourself bending over or changing things to suit your clients, this is a people pleasing pattern.
4. **Not enough time** - You can't get everything done you want and need to get done. Therefore, you're constantly feeling the pressure of not having enough time.
5. **Perfectionism** – Needing it to be perfect or all your ducks in a row before putting it out there, often spending way more time on things than you need to, and feeling stressed when it's not working out the way you want it to.
6. **Self-doubt** – This happens when you are second guessing yourself. When you are feeling fear of being seen and out there. Another way this shows up is feeling like a fraud or worried about getting it "wrong" somehow.
7. **Addicted to busyness** - Having a belief that if you are busy, then you're productive. You choose busyness over recharging. A symptom of this being that your work/life balance is also *OUT* of alignment. You may just be easily distracted and unorganized. This is also the person who works harder and not so much smarter. Without your busyness, you don't know your value or purpose, so you NEED it to feel important or valued somehow.

- How are all of those impacting your relationship? Can you see where you are having the same issues in your relationship? This is a good time to really ponder how your business is truly affecting your relationship and see if you can reveal any others not listed above.

- Now identify all the beliefs, sabotaging patterns, damaging behaviors, intense emotions (which are generally signs of unhealed baggage) that make up your "inner world". Are they at the root of all the above issues and challenges? Can you see where they are crossing into these areas or others?

It's the deeper level, inner world stuff above that you REALLY need to focus on first and foremost. The area it's showing up in is just the symptom. Sometimes it shows up more easily in one area, making it easy to identify. Which is why looking at *all* of them is so important if you are going to truly live the full dream life you have on your vision board, and more.

The subconscious (automatic) destructive and damaging behaviors, patterns, thoughts and emotions are the biggest factors preventing you from a deeper and passionate connection with your partner. They're preventing stronger boundaries with your partner and your clients. They prevent trust and confidence in yourself to ask for what you want and the ability to receive everything you are deserving and worthy of (specifically love, support and financial flow). They prevent you having FAITH in something bigger than you. Call that God, Source, Creator, whatever; a solid faith in something is what will give you a solid foundation for certainty and "knowing" when everything outside of you looks uncertain.

Once you address this deeper level inner world stuff, the rest is skills, strategies and ways of BEING! Communication, relating skills, time management, energy and soul alignment, genius-aligned marketing and growth strategies, and a well-developed intuition are the results you get by addressing this deeper level.

When it comes to relationships for entrepreneurs, there can be a few additional challenges. The entrepreneurial journey is not an easy one, right?!? We have to learn so many things, wear multiple hats and become a "jack-of-all-trades" to get a business off the ground. Often we are having to pivot fast and learn something new while implementing it simultaneously. I used to say I got good at flying the plane while building it at the same time!

There are times where we need to spend long days doing what needs to be done, but it's meant to be sprints; short periods of long hours. Then have some recharge time before another sprint. Being in full divine flow makes this possible. The problem I see most is, entrepreneurs stay in constant sprint mode. Since a relationship is a living entity between 2 people, it gets neglected for too long, then dies, damaging both people in the process.

If you are in a relationship with another entrepreneur, the typical trap is that you BOTH spend so much time talking about business, supporting each other, bouncing ideas off each other, or just working. That's because you both understand the other's passion and purpose, so you start to forget about putting that same level of focus and energy into your love partnership. When it's all work and no play, guess what happens?

For those not in a relationship with another entrepreneur it can be hard for non-entrepreneurial partners to truly understand what it takes to "make it" and while they are being as supportive as they can, it can be a hard road for them too.

No matter what, for your relationship to be EPIC, you need:

1. Excellent communication skills
2. Ample quality time (this doesn't mean loads of actual time)
3. Knowing each other's Love and Connection Language
4. A highly satisfying and orgasmic sex life – or at least be on the same page
5. Knowing how to flow and pivot with life's phases, storms and curveballs (being good at adapting to change together)
6. To work as a TEAM, sharing the load, supporting each other
7. Shared values, vision and desire to encourage each other in the pursuit of living their unique purpose
8. A high level of emotional maturity, emotional intelligence

and self-awareness (this means working on healing your baggage)
9. Healthy boundaries and taking personal responsibility
10. Fun, adventures, playtime

And to have a thriving business you need:

1. Excellent communication skills
2. Ample quality time to focus on doing the important parts of the business
3. Excellent time and resource management – knowing how to work smarter, not harder
4. Knowing how to connect to, and serve your clients
5. Knowing how to flow and pivot with business phases, storms and curveballs (adapting to change again)
6. Have a TEAM – this means releasing some control, stepping up into being a leader, delegating to share the load and support each other
7. A clear vision, mission and values
8. A high level of emotional maturity, emotional intelligence and self-awareness (working on healing your baggage again)
9. Healthy boundaries and taking personal responsibility – including around work and home time!
10. Fun, adventure, and playfulness
11. Genius aligned strategies for marketing and growth
12. Knowing how to get into a divine FLOW state, and utilize your intuition for decisions

Can you see how a big chunk of these overlap? If you find that in your business you're good at something like taking personal responsibility, or you are better at boundaries but not in your relationship, or vice versa, you need to ask yourself why? Then address that so you can thrive in all areas.

Something magical happens when you have such a rocking relationship! One where you feel deeply loved, completely supported, blissfully happy, ultimately confident, excited by the future, fueled with passion and purpose, feeling playful and adventurous, all because your partner inspires this in you.

When you bring this high level of energy (aka a high vibration), inner security, abundance and optimism into your business, this is the basis for that state of "divine flow"! Being in a divine flow state is how you attract and see the high ROI opportunities to accelerate your business success without taking more out of you, the opportunities you don't get guided to and can't see when you are stressed, overwhelmed, frustrated or low energy (aka low vibration).

Being in that divine flow state is the magic in the business growth that creates the time and energy to put into yourself (self-care) AND your relationship so those areas can thrive. That energy fills your heart and soul with goodness. That then fuels your divine flow state. Can you see how this works now?

Your relationship is the key!

Being so close to your heart and deeply personal, it has the power to reveal your hidden saboteurs – the inner baggage and patterns currently damaging and draining everything else. This is where your biggest transformation opportunity lives, unlocking everything you dream of if you choose to face it and go there. Abundant love, happiness, peace, prosperity, fun, passion and the freedom from having all of your needs met is completely possible for you.

If you have your relationship, your business, and your health, all absolutely rocking, congrats and well done! If you don't, I have a gift for you.

I wrote a short ebook, "Relationship Savers: A Guide to Having an EPIC Relationship and a Thriving Business!" It takes 15 – 20 mins to read. Unless you're Speedy Gonzales; then it could be less. It expands on some of this. It's interactive and also shares more detail. From there you'll be offered a free 30 minute "Relationship And Business Impact Call" or "Clarity Call" so you can talk to me directly about your situation. During this time, I will share any insights and quick solutions I can give to start making things a lot better for you both.

I just want to see more entrepreneurs absolutely kicking ass in their business without killing their relationship in the process. I want to see them transforming their business so they gain more of the rewards from it, instead of burning out and destroying themselves trying to get there.

We really can have it all! The question is, do you really want it, and are you committed to doing what it takes to have it?

Investing in another business program or strategy isn't going to help unless you get your relationship and inner world sorted. Everything else divine FLOWS from there and I can show you how.

You know where to find me!

Scan or click on the above QR code to claim your bonus gifts and free resources from the featured authors! qrco.de/bcrTuK

Chapter 3

Laura Inspire

Within 5 mins, my life changed!!!

I cannot count the number of moments, even if I closed my eyes, how many times that my life has taken a HUGE UNEXPECTED LIFE CHANGE!

Just by having a 5 minute conversation can change your WORLD!

BAM!!! It's the feeling you feel when you hear the news, minute by minute passing by, as you allow the news to REALLY set in. As you take stock of what just happened. You then start to prepare yourself for what is next!! How will your life ever be the same?

Life doesn't STOP, just because of what just happened to you. The clock keeps ticking... tick, tick, tick.

How do you ever recover and move forward from this? That's the question that keeps repeating in your head. Life deals you all kinds of problems. It's how you work through them that counts. Minute by minute, day by day.

Recently, I had one of those UNEXPECTED LIFE CHANGES that hit me in the face. BAM!!! It left me with nothing in my tank to give, to be there for others, or to even take care of my daughter.

· · ·

Every day felt hard, my life purpose fell away. I was left questioning everything, as I lay in bed, trapping myself in those four white walls.

The best advice came one day from a wise woman who encouraged me to FOCUS on just one activity per day. It didn't have to be big. It could be as simple as making the bed, getting some sunshine for 5 minutes, or maybe a little walk. It was all a process about GETTING ME STARTED!!

Day by day, it became easier to look at the little 5 minute blocks of time, as they felt light and achievable. This method gave me back direction in my day without feeling overwhelmed. In my present state of mind, I knew that anything that felt hard, I was never going to do. It had to be easy, achievable and have a light feeling about it, in order for me to take action.

The days got easier as life went on, but I knew I was still struggling with my feelings. I felt like I was carrying around the heaviest backpack of emotions, hurt feelings, stress, and trauma. It was time!!

Time to change my approach towards life. I was ready to start the process of letting go of what didn't serve me anymore. What I no longer wished to have in my life!

It was time to unpack that backpack!

I was so tired and exhausted from carrying this extra weight on my shoulders for what seemed like an eternity.

Can I ask you this? Are you carrying one of those heavy backpacks? Is it time for you to let go of what's inside?

I set foot on my personal journey of unpacking all the past hurts and experiences while learning the art of healing myself. Like any journey, we can't do this alone, so I enrolled in a support team. Mentors, coaches, family, friends and even my very caring daughter (wise beyond her years). What I thought would be a quick journey has taken me months. Layer by layer, I slowly unpacked my backpack. There were years of past experiences and hurts that had never been released and let go of. It now feels so much lighter!

Is it empty yet??

NOPE, it will always be a work in progress, as I continue to swap those heavy emotions for all the love and laughter that I can possibly squeeze in there!! We are NOT looking to create a PERFECT LIFE, but one of progress towards a more meaningful, fulfilling life that we can be proud of! Throughout my healing process, I have taken those wise words from my friend (who shared to focus on just one activity per day). From this I created, **'The 5 Min Method'**.

What is The 5 Min Method?

JUST GET STARTED!!!

Everything in life always feels TOO HARD until we get started.

From a very young age, I learnt to take action in 5 minute blocks. Mum used to call me a "5 minute wonder" as a child. 5 minutes playing with this, and then wanting to move to the next set of toys 5 minutes later. This continued all day long. It drove her crazzzzzy!!!

As I got older, I learned about the "cause and effect" method. I gave everything a go and fell on my face sooooooooo many times. But quickly, I learned what worked and what didn't. I didn't want to be held back with the fear of, "what if I didn't take action"!!

Without ever getting started, how would you know if you could create new habits, achieve those plans you set for yourself, or enjoy what life has to offer you along the way?

5 minutes is the MAGIC NUMBER that allows you to move forward without feeling overwhelmed or having to commit too much time!

Think about it, if I was to ask you to start a new habit, and said that you had to spend 20 minutes a day to implement it, what emotions would this bring up for you?

- You might take action right away, seeing the true value of what this new habit could do for you.
- Most people would find an excuse to not act at all.
- Time is often the biggest excuse! Most people don't think they have 20 minutes to invest in themselves per day.
- It could take them up to a month to see the value of this, or some may NEVER ever get started at all!!

As you can see, the hardest part is always getting STARTED. Why not make it so small (achievable) that you just can't fail!!!

· · ·

5 minutes is the Magic Number which allows you to take ACTION, without the FEAR of FAILURE, or the excuse of being TIME POOR!

Everyone has 5 minutes to spare in their day, correct?

- Once you allow yourself the space to get started, set a 5 minute timer on your phone.
- This will allow you to apply the new habit or focus on the task that needs to be achieved.
- Just watch how your resistance drops away, and you get lost in time.
- You then reset the timer for another 5 minutes and repeat the process.
- Before you know it, you have done 20 minutes without even knowing it.

Can you see the benefits and how much easier it would be to continue with this process?

The key to success: Just Get Started!!

"Within just 2 weeks of being part of The 5 Min Method Program, I have felt a greater sense of calm and much less anxiety. This has led me to being more productive and feeling less overwhelmed throughout the day!"
   Sarah
   (Perth, WA)

What is The 5 Min Method program?

I'll take you on a journey over 6 weeks, where you will discover how to reduce the heavy burden that you have been carrying throughout your life, and replace it with love and laughter.

We'll break down the journey into stages, which will allow you to uncover how to create a more meaningful life by filling your backpack with the right tools.

DECODER:

Backpack = What you're carrying around - like thoughts, emotions, baggage, hopes, achievements and so much more

- When your backpack overflows with heavy negative emotional rocks, we become rundown, sick and tired
- Fill the backpack with positive emotions, thoughts, joy, love, happiness and you can create a more meaningful life

Journey = How we see our life - at what stage are we?

"When you have exhausted all possibilities, remember this: YOU HAVEN'T!!"

Stage 1 of the Journey - Release & Let Go
How heavy is your backpack... is it weighing you down?
Are you ready to "Let Go" of what is not serving you?
Is it fear, doubt, overwhelm, or perhaps some Mum guilt?
What will it take for you to let go of these burdens (heavy rocks in your backpack)?
It's time to declutter your mind and release those burdens you have been carrying and invite more love and laughter into your life.
Are you ready?
Stage 2 of the Journey - Invite In
Once you have started to unpack and release the heavy emotional burdens in your backpack, it is now time to 'Invite In'.
Now you have space in your backpack to fill it up with joy, happiness, and all the things that you welcome in to create a more meaningful life.
What does this look like for you?
Stage 3 of the Journey - Road Bumps
How many times have you hit a road bump in your life and struggled to know what to do?
Who do you turn to for support?
What would your next step look like?
How quickly could you move through this, so that you don't stay stuck in your own shit for days!
I'll teach you the 4 methods that have always worked for me, which will allow you to move closer to create a more meaningful life for you!

· · ·

Stage 4 of the Journey - Trust the Process

> "You can't connect the dots looking forward; you can only connect them looking backwards. So you have to trust that the dots will somehow connect in your future." - *Steve Jobs*

Life is about trusting it will all work out in the end. Yes, we do need to have some direction, but we also must trust in the process that it all happens for a reason!

Creating FOCUS and TRUST is the next step.

Learning to surrender is one of the hardest lessons you may need to learn. TRUSTING your intuition allows you to be guided throughout the day. This invites flow into your life. When we are in a state of flow, life becomes easier and more meaningful!

Stage 5 of the Journey - Take Action Now!

What's your purpose? Or have you lost your direction in life?

Is goal setting exciting for you?

I've never loved planning out months in advance. This method left me feeling heavy.

What if you could create POSITIVE FOCUS with ACTION STEPS?

Where focus goes, energy flows!!!

This method allows you to work on what you chose to 'Invite In' + Focus + Action Steps = Creating a More Meaningful Life with Energy!!

Stage 6 of the Journey - Reward Yourself!

How is your backpack feeling now?

Reward is the best gift that you can give yourself!!!

I am a BIG believer that you should reward yourself daily, weekly, monthly, or whenever you feel like it!!!

Set yourself a FOCUS or something you wish to achieve. Then right after that, set yourself a REWARD (big or small) and take the ACTION to achieve it!!

WHY do you have to wait to be rewarded by someone else?

Why not reward yourself!!!

By now it's time to Celebrate your backpack success!

Over the last 5 weeks, you have invited in new tools that supported you in creating a more meaningful life!

Are you ready to join me in a 'happy dance'?

The 5 Min Method to a More Meaningful Life started as my own personal journey to recovering from an UNEXPECTED LIFE CHANGE and now is having a momentous rippling effect with my clients.

In just a short space of time, Anna has seen a transformation with her own emotions and approach to creating a more meaningful life for her and her family.

Reading Anna's journey below makes me feel all warm and fuzzy!

"Laura introduced me to **The 5 Min Method** through my mentoring sessions. She guided me through each week and shared the method that would support me on my journey.

I was at a crossroads in my life, having relocated interstate with my family. I was wanting change, a chance to discover myself and work out how to create the life I wanted for my family.

Just taking 5 mins in a day to focus on one thing I wanted to work towards has taken away the feelings of overwhelm I was having. I have even created more time for myself, which now allows me the capacity to give to others.

The accountability Laura gave to me throughout the mentoring program was so valuable. She's so encouraging & always gave practical solutions to any road bumps I had along the way.

I was feeling lost (& very home sick). Now I'm feeling more focused on what's important to me, more peace in the day-to-day life & I'm so hopeful for my family & my future".

Anna (Melbourne, Victoria)

In order to cross the finish line, I would love you to:

Raise your right hand, take it behind your left hand shoulder, and give yourself a good pat on your back!!!

Congratulations you have finished this leg of your journey :-)

Lastly, where will your next journey take you?

Just like Sarah and Anna, you too can use **The 5 Min Method** to create a more meaningful life with a backpack overflowing with love and laughter!

Where is my journey now?

After months of putting into practice **The 5 Min Method** for myself, I now have purpose back in my day!

Releasing and letting go of all those past negative emotions I had stuck in my backpack has allowed me to fly! I feel so much lighter, happier, and more grounded. You could say my backpack is overflowing with love and laughter.

If it wasn't for the UNEXPECTED LIFE CHANGE, and my ability to trust the process of surrendering, I wouldn't have been able to connect the dots looking backwards!! Life is a journey..

Applying **The 5 Min Method** will give your life more direction!

What's in your Backpack??

Laura Inspire -

Creator of The 5 Min Method

Scan or click on the above QR code to claim your bonus gifts and free resources from the featured authors! qrco.de/bcrTuK

Chapter 4

Verena Boeheim ~ Intuitive Mentor

MY MESSY LIFE PATH

I closed my eyes and took a deep breath, trying to will away the tears that were threatening to fall. I was so tired of feeling this way. Every day felt like a battle, and I was losing more ground than I was gaining. I had started my day with such good intentions, but somehow, everything went wrong. I tried to focus on my coffee, letting the warmth of the mug seep into me, but it was no use. The darkness inside of me was too strong.

I felt numb and hopeless. Like everything was pointless. I wanted to give up. To just crawl back into bed and let the world go on without me. But I knew that wasn't an option. I had responsibilities.

We all have a certain amount of courage and fearlessness inside us, but sometimes it's hard to unleash that inner strength.

I had been pretending to be someone else for so long; I had forgotten who I was. Or maybe I never even knew. It was easier to hide behind a mask than to face the possibility of being rejected. And it was also exhausting. Every day, I would wake up and put on a show, pretending to be someone that I wasn't.

· · ·

One day, something changed. I realized I didn't need to be someone else. — I could just be myself. That was when everything changed for me. It was scary at first, but it was also liberating. Finally, I felt like I could breathe again.

We are often told that to be successful, we must struggle. We must work hard for what we want in life. But what if that's not true? What if the key to a happy and fulfilling life is finding out what you really want and going for it?

In this chapter, we will explore the idea of finding your way back to your Authentic Self.

Are you ready to stop struggling and start living?

It was only when I decided to start living by my human design that everything changed.

I began to question what society had taught me about life and happiness. I started to look within and ask myself what it was that I really wanted in life. Guess what? It wasn't anything that could be found within the confines of my job or relationships. I wanted to travel and see new places. I wanted to learn and explore new ideas. I wanted to connect with people on a deeper level and share my Authentic Self with them.

Corporate life was a living hell for me. The job put me in a dark depression. I avoided confronting who I was. That only seemed to increase my feelings of isolation in this world that felt like nobody cared about anyone or anything except themselves.

Every day for years on end, all that would come to mind was, "I'm not good enough." My life had become one big facade — a smile plastered across my face while going about my day because there wasn't anything else left worth living for.

I lived a life of illusion, believing that if only I could find the right person to love, then my pain would disappear. It was never-ending and ultimately led me down an even darker path, with no relief in sight.

For two decades, I lived a sad and painful life as an excuse-maker. I carefully chose all my romantic relationships to escape depression — but they never worked out.

It took me a long time to recognize that my relationship with food, exercise, and stress was not healthy either. It was a vicious cycle. I would end one, only for another addiction: overeating, overworking, or spending money on things I didn't need to fill the void created by an inauthentic life.

Pushing myself to be a high achiever and people-pleaser seemed like just another way I could fall deeper into depression. It never occurred to me that "pushing" might be the problem.

I lived in a state of carefully crafted lies for years, avoiding the shadows and cracks that were present within myself. It was much easier to spend money on clothes I didn't need when my depression began, as an escape from having those uncomfortable feelings. At first, it seemed like fun but eventually became self-destructive because nothing could ever fill this deep wound inside me.

When the pain was too much, I would rather escape, and seek temporary relief with yet another bottle of Prosecco than face what might happen if I felt my feelings. The depression itself felt so drastic that asking myself, "What's on the other side?" was not worth risking everything for a few minutes of peace at home or work when I could just avoid these demons altogether.

I had been running from them for so long. Crying myself to sleep every night.

Feeling like a fraud in my work environment felt normal, and it became an everyday routine. The higher I climbed up the corporate ladder, the less connected I was with people around me. Everything felt fake, including relationships at home or among friends.

One night, choking on my tears while crying in my pillow, it suddenly occurred to me that this is what life feels like when you hit rock bottom. You do not recognize any of your reality anymore because everything has changed so much for the worse. There have even been times when suicide seemed appealing.

The darkness felt like it was closing in on me, and I couldn't breathe.

The pressure to be perfect started choking me. I was so scared that people would find out what a fraud I was. I was trapped under layers of lies, telling myself negative things so naturally, they became my mindset; wearing masks every day without even realizing what I was hiding behind.

Once my tears ceased, I just lay there in exhaustion. My eyes were closed, waiting for the Universe to take me home, to end this life for me. The life where I felt unwanted, unrecognized, unloved, unseen, and unappreciated.

I was screaming, calling out for someone or something to help me. I pleaded with God. I made deals with him, asking him to take me back, telling him that this was the end for me. I did not have any more strength or willpower left.

I lay there and waited.

My tears dried.

An unknown calm filled my heart and soul.

I felt something I have never felt before.

An inner voice softly said, "Your time has not yet come. Get up. Be joyful. Live your life. Be you."

I stood up, went to the desk in my living room, and made a bucket list of what I wanted. I wrote intentions and the next steps to pull myself out of desperation and depression.

I was finally going to take charge of my life. No more would I be a victim. No longer would the voice in my head get louder and stronger with negative thoughts about myself. I've had it! The time had come when all this negativity started feeling too much like reality, so instead, I made the decision to create an authentic life.

After my journey through depression and unhealthy habits, I discovered that it was time to stop holding back. When you listen to your inner voice, it leads the way toward a fulfilling life full of joy and happiness.

I found myself in an unauthentic rut with no meaning or fulfillment until one day when all clicked into place. This experience gave me clarity on what kind of person I wanted to be. I discovered that ignoring my inner voice was the source of my unhappiness and eventually, my breakdown.

I left my high-paying corporate job, put all my belongings into storage, and accepted a friend's offer to work as a relief hotel manager for an island resort in the Kingdom of Tonga.

I spent more time with myself. My true Authentic Self was starting to come out. It was like a switch had been flipped, allowing for new opportunities that before were not available because of the way I approached life from an intellectual level, rather than an emotional one. The months in Tonga have seen such positive changes in everything: work performance; mental clarity (especially regarding stress); improved relationships - even friendships starting up again after being stagnant.

It was a slow process, but I allowed myself this freedom so much that it became part of who I am now because there's no one else telling us how we should be living our lives, anyway! And after a while, everything shifted around until all these new feelings weren't crazy anymore. Instead, they felt natural.

Finally, I was living from the heart rather than following society's standards. Life started flowing more easily and everything just felt right in my world again!

When I returned home after six months, I felt free to be me.

Life is an accumulation of experiences. While some might seem positive and wonderful, they are not the same as living authentically with all your heart. It can be difficult when things don't always go our way or turn out how we planned for them to happen in this world where everything happens so fast! But there's one thing worth noting: You needn't wait around until something terrible happens before feeling alive.

Today I write, travel, spend time in nature with my dog. I live by my human design, listen to my intuition, explore my surroundings, and share my tips on connecting with our intuition and finding a way back to our true Authentic Self through intuitive mentoring, books, social media, magazine articles and podcast interviews.

I created my social media presence as an easily accessible online destination for motivation, connection, and education on a variety of topics. These center around intuition and human design with lots of inspiration, motivational tips, and foolproof tools to help others to create an authentic life by design.

There is nothing more rewarding for me than to see the impact I can have by being my true Authentic Self and seeing how it inspires others to be real, too.

· · ·

By sharing myself with others, I find it gives all of us an opportunity to affect the world together as we move to a more authentic, transparent, and loving place.

Life is a holistic experience, and it doesn't just happen to you.

It is a path of self-discovery, and it will lead you in the direction where happiness can be found, even if only for moments at first and maybe not always those. The journey may seem difficult, but remember that everything worth doing usually has some degree of difficulty attached!

It's time to live your dreams.

The message I share with the world comes from my own journey of finding happiness in life, which has been an arduous one filled with desperation and depression.

The message I share is about authenticity and purpose and living your dreams and being true to yourself so you can be of the highest service to the world.

I have learned to see the beauty in every situation, no matter how difficult it may be. My goal is always on pursuing joy and happiness and living an authentic life by design.

Life may throw us curveballs, but that doesn't mean we should give up on our dreams. I learned the beauty in all my situations and want to share it with other people so they can too!

The changes that have come in fruition in my life are something you can also achieve with some work and dedication! It takes a lot of self-reflection to understand what makes us happy in this world, but when people tell us how great things are going for them after they make their dreams happen, well, let me just say:

YOU CAN DO IT TOO!

There isn't anything stopping any one person from living their authentic life.

You can explore any opportunity available without fear if only you choose to do whatever feels right now.

No matter where you are in life, what your circumstances may be, all of us want one thing: Happiness. It's something we can all achieve with some guidance from within ourselves, plus whatever help comes our way along this journey called "life".

I was once at rock bottom until I rediscovered my intuition and found Human Design, which led me back to my true Authentic Self and helped ease stress through calmness and contentment.

I'm here to tell you it is possible for everyone, no matter where they are in life or what resources or advantages they have been given. All we truly want as human beings on this earth is peace and happiness, but too often our pursuit of these things leads us down dark paths which only serve painful ends like stress and anxiety instead of joy-filled fulfillment.

I teach people how to find true contentment by listening to their intuition and creating an authentic life by design.

Through my "IHCA" approach: Intuition | Human Design | Clarity | Action, I share the tips and secrets I used to pull myself out of depression and into a place of pure love, excitement, and joy. By first clearing our space physically, mentally, and spiritually, we create a space for our dreams and goals to manifest into reality. Living an authentic life and achieving our dreams is not a challenge when we remove the blocks to authenticity and seek it from within.

The journey to finding happiness is a personal one, but once you do find your way, there's no turning back. I spent my entire life looking for it on the outside until one day it finally hit me: happiness lies within us at every moment!

The dreams of my life came true when I finally believed in myself. Now, every moment is an amazing experience because there are no limits to what I can achieve!

Life is a series of adventures and I want to help others navigate their way through the day-to-day. It's daring to take risks for what you really believe in, but we all owe it to ourselves to be able to love life without feeling like something is missing - authenticity makes us happy.

As I made my way through the pain and rage, one thing that never left me was hope. Hope for a better life; hope in knowing what is right from wrong; hoping against all odds because there's more than this small world we live in. No matter how bad things seem right now, we have the power over our own fates! With practice comes improvement and soon enough, you will see just like me: your path becomes clear once again.

. . .

You are capable of anything if only given the opportunity.

Life is an adventure, and I've found my voice.

After years spent struggling from addiction to depression over what seemed like the bleakest prospects for myself ever — I finally woke up from this nightmare, only to find that life can be even more amazing than you imagined possible!

Life is a precious gift.

My focus has always been on helping people all around the world, through my writing and intuitive mentoring, to create authentic lives that they love living in! I offer tools for motivation as well as courage so you can follow your heart's desire without getting stuck along the way, because we all need some help sometimes.

Are you ready to activate your dream life and to live an authentic life by design?

I thought so.

Let's dive into this together now.

Scan or click on the above QR code to claim your bonus gifts and free resources from the featured authors! qrco.de/bcrTuK

Chapter 5

Cori Stuart ~ Holistic Healing

"Self-trust is the first secret of success."
  Ralph Waldo Emerson

I have always been an individual who believes that no matter the situation in life, one should live life from the soulful heart instead of the logical mind. As a result of this concept, most of my life I have been told to stop being so sensitive, to learn to be tougher or thicker skinned, to bottle up most sides of my personality, to stop being emotional or weak, and go with the flow.

Nowadays, this is the stereotypical story of an individual we know as an empath. After decades of stuffing ourselves down, many of us feel disconnected, burned out and fearful, and numb and unloved. Heck, it's most of the human race thanks to the current world events.

Thankfully, many of us have decided the world provides enough disconnection, and decided to connect with the world in a different way. It's time to reconnect to ourselves. There is a lot of hype regarding self care, reconnection, and flipping the script from people pleaser to implementing self care into our lives.

What does self-care truly mean? Is it as simple as massages and repeating affirmations? I don't think so. I think self care is something much deeper and involves self-trust, and my client's results of connected alignment exemplify this. But what does connected alignment or self-trust truly mean? According to *Psychology Today*, self trust is the firm reliance on the integrity of yourself. From this definition, self trust sounds a lot like sovereignty, or freedom from external control. As we're shifting from numb and fearful, how do we embody being a self trusting and sovereign soul?

Let's side step a little bit from self care, trust and sovereignty, and learn more about the importance of the seat of the soul known as the heart. This is the place of balance, integration, and trust, especially sovereign trust (and the shadow side of the heart, people pleasing & codependency). Physically, the heart is one of the first organs developed in our body. It has double the connections to the brain than the brain does to the heart. Talk about important. Without the heart, the rest of the physical body will not develop and cannot function.

Additionally, science is catching up with what many cultures have known for thousands of years. Studies are showing the body has three brains within; one being the physical brain, and the other two being the heart and the gut. If one of the brains is out of balance, the rest of the body cannot balance and will experience dis-ease throughout.

Physically, when the heart is out of balance, our body systems can produce symptoms or dis-eases such as heart attacks, anxiety, breast cancer. Our immune system becomes compromised, which can lead to skeletal and muscular issues. For not being a physical brain, the heart is crucial to existence and yet we burrow much of our hurt or trauma within the heart, lungs or other systems. These are classified within the heart chakra realm. We accept the physical issues as status quo until we reach such a high level of living from fear and numbness that we own the decision to shift and live from a different perspective.

Energetically, the heart is the crossroad of the upper and lower chakras. According to most systems, it is the center for the integration of the masculine and the feminine, and physical action combining with divine energetic connection. Combining with intellect, if our heart is not balanced, our emotions cannot be balanced and the ability to think clearly is compromised, i.e. healthy boundaries in relationships and self trust disintegrates, and the shadow side of self trust, codependency, has room to develop.

Back on track, how do we achieve the foreign concept of self-trust now that we are done feeling disconnected and/or codependent? Many of us have tried Western medicine only to find ourselves either in worse mental shape, needing more medicine to take care of the physical side effects, spending years on a couch, reading numerous books, or coaching programs with few results. When we find ourselves in such a state, we normally have a different teacher, reading, or friend appear suggesting we try something deeper, something truly soulful and holistic, better known as treating the whole person, not just treatment of the symptoms or the surface level.

The beauty of living life from the heart, when we flip from living for others, feeling not worthy, and playing small, we have the opportunity to live for ourselves, to be divinely connected and aligned, and to be loved, even through our weakest moments. Let's learn a few techniques on how to accomplish this.

Working with individuals in learning more about themselves through the chakras and towards living life through love, and reconnecting with their soul song through energetic, physical, and intellectual techniques is the foundation of my practice. Several of these techniques include learning to trust their own gut instincts. Including establishing boundaries, not walls, and living and speaking our truth from the heart. Then to step through fear while opening and maintaining the gateway for divine connection. Holistically reconnected, self loving, empowered, and loved in spite of ourselves. What a pleasant script flip from disconnected, numb, and unloved.

The beautiful part of healing is there are so many tools or techniques we can incorporate into our daily lives. We begin by going deep, assessing where the blocks are within the body, especially the heart, preventing connection from our elusive self-trust and worth; *Hello boundaries.* One of the techniques we use is to own what is taking space between their ears, i.e. what is their truth versus the opinions of others, which do not serve their purpose. Then how they can clear the garbage out and open space for better opportunities using mindset and energy work?

Most of our thoughts are a conglomerate of our parents' knowledge, including their circle of influence and the lessons they learned from their parents - normally six to seven generations back. In releasing what no longer serves us, we create space for healing and growth. A simple example of this is the type of products we buy, a simple example being cars. If your grandmother bought Ford, your parents probably bought Ford, and more than likely, at one point, you may have owned a Ford as well.

Furthermore, the words we utter are the repetition of what we have learned through thought.

> Iyanla Vanzant states it best, "speaking from the heart means sharing the truth of your being... not only will your truth set you free, but it will also liberate you from guilt, shame, and fear."

Definitely worth breaking the fear cycles for that type of liberation and understanding. One of the most important intellectual techniques we can incorporate into our lives is truthful thinking. This means being able to step out of the situation, remove the emotion and judgment, and ask what is the truth of the situation. Then take action accordingly. It is ownership of acting on the truth, not who is right or wrong, and not acting or living in fear or guilt. Talk about perspective shift. This is the first step towards transformation of self ownership and bringing bliss back into your own life.

An additional technique in developing and owning self-trust is forgiveness. Forgiveness is one of the strongest and most empowering actions we can embody through life on both the intellectual and the spiritual fronts. Forgiving others brings our power back by removing victim status by removing their control, as does forgiving yourself.

> As Caroline Myss states:
> "The liberation that forgiveness generates comes in the transition to a higher state of consciousness - not just in theory, but energetically and biologically."

You do not have to reach out to the other individual to accomplish forgiveness. I am a huge fan of taking pen to paper and writing out what needs forgiven, or what no longer serves you, and burning it. I encourage clients to do this on a regular basis, as often as monthly with the full moon or as infrequently as the solstice or time changes. As an energy practitioner, I also perform energetic cord cutting and balancing to assist in release. Let the universe recycle what no longer serves you and create fertilizer for that which will assist your soul to dance.

Building on healing the energetic body, I utilize several different techniques blended with Reiki to reconnect and balance the heart and remove blocks. Reiki is a Japanese energy healing technique, which assists in balancing the body which utilizes the intentional movement of energy. Added bonus in using reiki, one does not have to re-endure the pain or inflammation to balance the imbalance from the body; nor to remember the incident for the body to release the stored memory. As a recipient of reiki, you get to take a meditative nap while the practitioner works with your energy to balance itself. As a practitioner, I assist in releasing current events in addition to past emotional or physical disease stored within the body, and in ending hereditary karmic cycles. Additionally, one of the aspects which my clients find advantageous is we can perform their sessions either by distance or in person.

I also incorporate reiki infused crystals and oils to assist in reconnection and release through the physical and the energetic bodies targeted for individual circumstances. I adore sharing their properties forward, and hearing success stories of these tools assisting individuals. Several benefits my clients have experienced are self-confidence, focus, abundance, and balance and bliss. One can incorporate crystals into one's daily life through sacred adornment, better known as jewelry, keeping in one's pocket or garments, having in one's room to shift the environment or arranging for different strategies within your space, or infusing water either to drink or bathe in too. Similarly, oils can also be worn on jewelry, used in lotions or elixirs. Oils can be taken internally (research your oils first), diffused, or used aromatically. How wonderful is it we can incorporate such items into spaces within our daily lives and amplify or dispel different factors from ourselves and the spaces around us?

On the physical level, we dive in with different ways to move the body and shift what's no longer of benefit. By addressing the different symptoms our body is showing, we have the holistic opportunity to understand what triggered the dis-ease, and more importantly, release the dis-ease. It's incredible when we tune into the whole body, past and present, and treat it as the whole instead of just one symptom or part. There is a reason why Western culture is shifting towards the cultural ways of the East which have been treating holistically for thousands of years. When the body is balanced, and our three brains are communicating in a healthy way, we no longer have to numb, hide from yourselves, or fail to trust your gut instincts.

When a person combines the intellectual, energetic and physical techniques to reconnect with the heart, opportunities abound to feel love and to be loved, to release the fears and embrace the confidence, to be weak while also empowered, and take action while being divinely connected. When we embrace every aspect of ourselves, including our sensitivities or our thin skin, we create space for balance and bliss within our own lives and space for our souls to dance. When the heart is energetically balanced, we have permeable boundaries and are able to give love to ourselves and others while also receiving love.

With intellectual perspective shift, we have better command of our worth, which shifts our relationships personally and professionally. As a result, we find ourselves finally taking action towards our dreams, towards starting our own career path, or higher paying jobs, and having less drama in our personal lives and relationships. One of my favorite examples of this is a client who went from a job she hated to a more aligned job which doubled her income, and she moved to the city of her dreams. These actions resulted as she released the voices of her parents, suggesting her unworthiness and stepped into her sovereignty, trusted her gut, and acted for her best interest.

Additionally, holistic healing provides the same opportunities for those around us. Two of the most enjoyable clients I have had the opportunity to work with involved two generations of women who shifted the way they relate with themselves by releasing codependency. While upgrading their intellectual space, one of the clients lost over ten pounds, and both decluttered the environments around them by releasing clothes and furniture, and taking better care of the physical structures they live in. Furthermore, both clients shifted the way they interact with other individuals by speaking from the heart, which created deeper family relationships and opportunities for better jobs. Both are living more in alignment with their soul dances, and I can't wait to hear how they continue to grow. The work these two have done has also created a ripple within the family such that others are not only taking note, but following their lead in creating boundaries through self-trust and heart centered action and creating space for their own opportunities.

Scan or click on the above QR code to claim your bonus gifts and free resources from the featured authors! qrco.de/bcrTuK

Chapter 6

Yesim Gura ~ The Business Co-Pilot

You have just been promoted to your dream job.

After years of working hard, building your knowledge and experience, nurturing relationships in various roles, companies, you are now in your first senior leadership role. This may be heading a function, a division, a business unit or a company as a General Manager, Managing Director or CEO. It may also be in the capacity of the CEO of the company you founded.

Whichever role it is, the key challenge you are now facing is that you need new skills and new perspective to succeed in your new role. The excitement of a promotion is great, however the new position comes with a number of challenges like;

- Feeling alone
- Feeling small
- Not knowing where and how to get started, how to get the support you need
- Being expected to have all the answers
- Being observed by many others
- Challenges from all directions and many contradictions to manage

- A very new and different agenda versus before, with many people and organization topics

How do I know ? I have been there...

At the age of 42, when I was first promoted to General Manager at a multinational company, I first felt a lot of joy, excitement and pride. I was the first local and female General Manager, also not coming from a more typical sales and marketing background. I had spent 16 years in roles in finance. Then, when I realized that I wanted to become a General Manager, I shared it with my manager, who then supported me by giving me a custom tailored Business Unit Director role so I could experience commercial skills. That role prepared me for the general management path. Here I was, a proud person, but very much alone. To make things worse, the previous General Manager had already left to another role in a different country and I was all by myself. On top, I had the added challenge of having been promoted from within. Meaning, I was now in a position to lead my peers from yesterday. Not easy; even a bit frightening. The business environment was also very tough with an economic downturn, need to restructure the company, organizational challenges and many more stuff going on.

The initial joy of the promotion did not last very long. Heading a business may look easy from the outside, but it is very different when you are in the leading position. It is a continuous struggle, balancing act, and everyone looks up to you, so the pressure is huge. The number of different agendas that you need to take care of, the multiple stakeholders, your team, and more. In the current times, the business environment is also getting more challenging owing to VUCA nature (volatile, uncertain, complex and ambiguous), new global risks (geopolitical, climate, pandemic) and new expectations (ESGT – Environmental/Social/Governance and Technology) from all leaders in the corporate world.

When I look back to those days, when I got that first true leadership role; wondering what would have made that journey easier and more successful, I have the answer; a mentor, or even better; a business coach. Someone who would be by my side to support me on the challenging journey; like a Business Co-Pilot. Wouldn't that be wonderful?

My answer is a big YES!

I was assigned a mentor and business coach only after 12 months in my new role. That was not timely enough. I wish I had had that opportunity starting from the beginning of my new appointment. Nevertheless, when we started working together with my business coach, it felt like a light was shed on the bumpy road in front of me. I could now see where I was going, when I had to take a turn, move faster or slow down. It was like having a reliable, experienced co-pilot next to me, whom I could trust, follow the advice, learn from and be able to discover my strength and potential by gaining back my confidence and courage.

Wouldn't you want a co-pilot by your side who would inspire, challenge and grow you at this important moment of your career?

After spending over 30 years in business and recently in the capacity of an Independent Board Member in a number of companies in different industries, I have found my life purpose in serving those executives in their first leadership journey. My coaching skills, combined with my business acumen and passion for serving, especially women on this path, makes me an actor of transformation and growth for my clients.

To give some examples of those transformations I have helped build:

An entrepreneur (solo), very smart, fast thinker, high achiever, carrying the whole load of the company she founded. As the CEO, she had to leverage her team, but first connect with them, understand them, and meet them where they were. So, we took her from where she was, to a position where she not only started practicing engagement, delegation, team spirit development and empowerment, but also helped grow her company several folds. The business roadmap we put together helped her think ahead, think big, and act stronger. Today, she has a very successful business run by a professional CEO, whereby she is focused on creating the next chapter.

Another founder and CEO, very successful in the tech Industry, with her company at a fast pace growth, as she would describe it "a different company every six months". She had many challenges to deal with; from day-to-day business to people, to strategic growth opportunities. Whenever there was a pivotal moment (and there were quite many indeed), I was there to help navigate and as she always said, "I was doing my magic". At the end, she told me, "you have been one of our key business pillars". Last year, her company went through a successful acquisition and we are now working on the transition.

A country managing director in a multinational company, who was promoted to lead in a culture very different from the one she was raised in, had many organizational and business challenges in her first year. At the end of that year, she said, "I couldn't have survived without your support". Now we are in our second year, which she calls "season two".

What I love about my work is that each case with each client is uniquely different and such a rewarding relationship for both sides. In a very short time, we build trust, respect, acceptance by all means.

On the business front, I add value thanks to my advantage of being "on the outside". This external view gives me the ability to ask the right questions that start turn on the engine of transformation and growth.

Here are some of those initial magic creating questions (so simple but so effective):

1. Tell me about yourself. A. Who are you? B. Where are you going?
2. What is wanted, needed or missing in your life?
3. Do you have a personal advisory board made up of five people?
4. When you have a mission to achieve, in what ways do you prevent yourself, block your success?
5. How could you prevent yourself from becoming a barrier to your own success?

Then, we go into business imperatives:

1. The why, how, and what of the business.
2. Understanding the business model.
3. The stakeholders and the connections.
4. Beyond the obvious; what is really happening – for this, I meet the team.
5. How to link all together, form the roadmap, ensure the

consistency of execution and stay agile on the bumpy roads ahead.

It is not a coincidence that there are five items on each list. I believe there is a magic in keeping it simple and focused.

Each session is different, custom tailored, full of surprises, discoveries. The commonality of all sessions is that they lead to a step towards self-discovery, strength and confidence, transformation that comes from inspiration, the will to succeed, and the toolbox to do so.

The result is leaders that feel more confident, capable, courageous and caring for their teams. We all need to be supported. The transformation starts the moment we recognize this fact and take action. The greatest strategies do not lead to success without the right execution plan and forward thinking. To achieve that at the top, you need to be inspired, challenged, and questioned by people you trust.

Trust is the beginning. Lasting relationships is the outcome. Success is then inevitable.

I believe each person deserves to discover their strength, feel supported, and be inspired.

If you feel inspired by my story and if you would like to discover your strength in your new challenges, I would love to offer you my leadership co-pilot guide to success.

Your Business Co-Pilot,

Yesim Gura

Thrive and Prosper

Scan or click on the above QR code to claim your bonus gifts and free resources from the featured authors! qrco.de/bcrTuK

Chapter 7

Tiffany Lorraine Galloway

The Resilient Mother
Redemption after a life of Heartbreak

What if YOU are just living when really YOU have the power to thrive?

When lockdown began, I looked down at my growing belly that now took over my lap. I couldn't get up. I had to rest. Two hours would pass this way. My elementary age girls from my failed marriage loved it because they finally had their pregnant, busy, full-time college student, mother's undivided attention. We made the most of it. But once it was quiet, and they were in bed, I was left to face myself for the first time in a long time. How did this happen? How did I get here? How does a good Christian girl end up a birth mother, divorced twice, then left pregnant single, and alone in the middle of a world pandemic of all things?

The answer was I had a pattern of behavior and choices that were not serving me. This was a brutal reality to face. Yet I was tired of attracting the same relationships, the same stories, the same drama, and the same co-dependency that kept me playing the victim of my own story. I took stock of my responsibility in the situation. I also had to give myself grace.

I was not given the tools, support, or resources needed to do any better than I did. But now I had the opportunity to change things. I had the opportunity to change the pattern of my life. I could establish my core values and live with integrity by finding myself for the first time in my life. For embracing my real truth and regain my intuition.

Providentially, I was taking a self-compassion class at my university. Fortunately, I had strong faith that God would be with me. Luckily, my love for my miracle son and sweet girls kept me motivated to stay calm as often as I could under the circumstances. You see, in some ways, I had been prepared for this. I had already been through difficult situations and heartbreak that nearly took my life. I knew that my life was meant for more. The story isn't over yet.

Trigger Warning (please note happened many years ago)

I looked in the mirror. I knew something had to change. Then I looked at the bed. There was a decision to be made at this moment because I realized if I continued not to eat for a few more days and laid back down in that bed, no one was going to do anything about it. So, did I want to live or not? I decided that I did and I never let my thoughts or emotions take me to the brink again.

Heartbreak, grief, and loss are part of life. You may have had more than your fair share, but life isn't fair, is it? You may have experienced emotional pain so great it became a physical sensation. You may have realized there was a choice to suffer in it or release it. Sometimes we need help in order to do this. We need validation, honesty, and empathy. I have seen it all. I am still here and I choose to thrive and so can you.

Success Story – Divorce Resolved in 12 Weeks

After gaining strength to move forward in my life, and adjusting to being a single mother of three, I began being mistaken as a coach online. At first, I laughed about it, but after this happened twelve times, I started paying attention.

As I was considering this path, I was asked to mentor a woman through her divorce. I was able to help Katie get through her divorce quickly within 12 weeks. I used my personal experience from divorce to help her take essential steps to take control of the situation.

Things like getting all the finances separated as quickly as possible prevented financial ruin. Creating a separation agreement until the divorce was legalized lead to less conflict. Preparing for single motherhood helped her make sure her children were secure in the transition into having two-parent homes. As I was able to validate different emotional reactions that came up on her journey, she was able to know she had options.

Katie said, "I could not have come this far without you".

She is doing so well now. She finished school, started dating again. Katie recently shared with me how much better life was being treated well in a relationship. This was a thrilling experience to know my mess could become a message that touched others' lives for the better. That every heartbreak I experienced would have the potential to create miracles and breakthroughs for other women. Now, as I look down at my son, who takes over my lap for cuddles, I know it was all worth it.

5 Healthy Coping Methods to A Resilient Mindset in the Face of Adversity:

1. **Self-compassion** – You are only human and that is okay. You are not alone in what you are feeling or experiencing. You are human and in life there are common human experiences like loss, grief, pain as well as joy, excitement, love... Your emotions are an automatic response to life; feelings are the meaning we put on the emotions you experience. You get to choose how you feel about the emotions you experience. You get to decide how you feel about yourself every day. Love yourself with grace, establish your core values to live with integrity, and accept yourself just as you are.

2. **Personal Development** – Take responsibility for your choices in life. Understand that if you don't like your life, the way that it is right now does not mean it has to stay that way. It is all up to you. It comes down to the daily habits,

lifestyle, and routines you are consistent with. Awareness is the first step to real change. Seek resources, mentors, and coaches for accountability to create a thriving lifestyle designed for you to become your personal best. Daily exercise, nutritious food, water, and good sleep are the basics. From there, you will decide what is important to you to grow.

3. **Affirmations** – In order to manifest the outcomes you desire, you must start creating the life you want with your words, thoughts, and actions. Where your focus goes, the energy flows – Tony Robbins. The mind believes everything you tell it. Be careful what you feed your mind, keep it positive and focused on what you really want to thrive.

4. **Gratitude Wall** – Every time something goes well, a prayer is answered, or a special memory is made, write it on post-it notes and stick them to a wall or board. Use this space to meditate, pray, or just pause. Even if all you only have 5 minutes a day, take that time to focus on what you have instead of what you lack. This will bring resilience through a perspective of appreciation for the little things in life. God's tender mercies are there when we choose to see them.

5. **Vision/Mission** – You get to create your life no matter what is going on because ultimately you are in control. You must create a clear vision for your future. It can be a vision board, writing down goals, time envisioning the future you want, etc. It is essential that you connect to your vision and mission daily to stay motivated. Leave the past behind, be in the present moment, and keep the vision of your dream future in front of you in order to empower yourself to create the life you desire to have.

This is the moment. Own it!

Mary Silver MSW

Scan or click on the above QR code to claim your bonus gifts and free resources from the featured authors! qrco.de/bcrTuK

Chapter 8

Julie Brown

Boost Your Business with Media Magic

It's what every business owner dreams of – a mention in the media. Online, print, radio, or TV – media matters. It's not just an acknowledgement that all your hard work has paid off and you've finally been recognized. Press coverage offers much more than an ego boost and recognition. It's truly transformational. And here's why:

- It helps you get your story heard. No matter what your business is, having the press talk about it will shout your message much louder and much further than any other marketing effort. Which means you get to help more people. Which is what we're all about, of course.
- Being in the media puts you in front of thousands of your ideal clients. By targeting publications and websites you know your clients are interested in, your story will go straight to the heart of those who are searching for someone like you to help them. Which of course means more sales.
- Building your brand helps grow your business. And with every mention in the media, it just keeps on growing.

- It gives you that all-important, sought-after expert status, which does wonders for your credibility in what you do. Fame and more earning power await you.

A bit about me

I wasn't always a journalist. In fact, I'd had a whole different career before my head was turned by the bright lights. I was an NHS professional, initially following my dream to be a nurse and work in psychiatry. I quickly progressed to senior management and also did a stint for the government inspecting hospitals around the UK. When you heard about NHS trusts being awarded star ratings (or losing them), that was me... for a while.

It was the death of my lovely mum that changed my focus and outlook on life. I wanted to do something different, something to get truly passionate about, and as I'd always enjoyed writing, I decided to become a journalist. Just like that – no training or experience. Getting a foot in the door wasn't easy, but when I did land my dream job, it was with a company who put time and effort into developing their staff, and I worked hard and soaked up everything they could teach me. I progressed to editor-in-chief quickly, followed by a big step-up to publisher – a role that combines the creative editorial side with the hard-nosed business part of running a group of magazines. I've been at it for 19 years now.

I started my entrepreneurial journey in 2017, training to be an accredited life coach before morphing into my current role as a visibility and media coach. I still do journalism as a freelancer and teach life coaching skills at a prestigious London Academy, too.

Put yourself ahead of the rest

I've noticed something over five years of my business journey. Entrepreneurs spend hours and hours bashing out content for social media, their blog, a YouTube channel or podcast. All of which is essential, and I teach it, of course. But there is a faster, more powerful way to create credibility and impact for your business. Media coverage is the supercharger for your visibility strategy.

Media coverage is available to every business owner, big or small, and it's free. Even the smallest of mentions in the media can do wonders for your bottom line. And guess what? Even though it's the most powerful form of marketing, and isn't really that hard to get involved with, only a fraction of business owners are using it. Be one of the ones that is and you'll rocket past your competitors.

This is what gets me out of bed on a morning. I want my clients to see the benefits of media coverage and embrace it as a fun way to get their message out there. Yes, be a little bit famous in their niche.

So, what could this newfound fame look like for you?

- You're changing more lives
- Your social media accounts have exploded
- Your web traffic is increasing
- Opportunities are landing at your feet
- You're making more sales
- You can finally put your prices up

Funnily enough, when I started my business, I had no intention of involving my journalist skills in it at all. In the end, after working with my first bunch of clients, the pull got too much. I knew it was something I needed to add in so I could help my future clients experience the type of success only media coverage can offer.

Don't just take my word for it. Meet Joanne Bridges:

I'll always remember child psychologist Joanne as she was the first person to sign up for my first online course, Six Weeks to Famous. Joanne was struggling to gain traction from her social media efforts and looking for a different way. Before she'd even finished the program, she had gone from brand new entrepreneur to in-demand expert, and a one-page feature in a magazine targeted right at her idea audience had added a considerable amount of money to her bank account. She'd gained her first piece of media coverage during week one, a short quote in Take a Break magazine.

Even I was impressed. Joanne had no previous experience of using media coverage in business but was motivated to make it work. She took on board my advice, implemented the training step by step, asked questions, took action and is still reaping the rewards today. You see, it's truly not that difficult. It's about knowing the correct strategy to follow and it's all there for you to enjoy. Joanne has never looked back and uses the power of the media on a weekly basis to continue to grow her client base.

Think you don't have anything to say? You're wrong.

My clients say this to me all the time. They think they can't snag a spot in the media as they have nothing useful to add. This is a piffle. We all forget how much we know and how many people there are who will benefit from our knowledge and expertise. New people enter your niche all the time, which makes repeating your message a must-do activity. You are an expert in what you do and if we're being really honest, you only need to be one step ahead of the people reading your copy to make it useful for them. We're all capable of this.

My client Gill McKay needed a bit of persuading, but she got there in the end. She was one of my "done for you'" PR clients and when I told her I wanted to feature her in Britain's number 1 equine magazine, she thought I'd lost my mind. You see, Gill is a coach who uses neuroscience in her work. What's that got to do with horses she asked me? Simple. The feature was about how to re-gain confidence after falling off a horse and confidence is one of Gill's specialties.

This is where the magic happens. Gill's niche is not horse riders, but by sharing the feature across all her platforms, she was telling her followers how much she knew about the subject. So much, in fact, that a magazine would hand over eight of their precious pages to her, which is priceless. It gave her credibility galore and hey presto, within a few days of someone (not a rider) seeing the feature online, they became a fully paid-up high-end client. When you become knowledgeable about using the media, and open up your mind to the possibilities, you'll find there are more opportunities than you can handle. You don't even need to be the best writer in the world. The journalists will correct any mistakes or re-jig if needed. Just get the words out of your head. That's all there is to it.

Want to give media coverage a go? Consider this:

* Talk about your customers, not your business: When was the last time you bought a magazine to read an article about someone's business? Me neither. How many times have you bought a magazine to read an article about a subject that is close to your heart,and found that what makes the article so compelling are the comments and insight from the experts they interviewed? Me too. And finally, how many of those experts managed to get a teeny, tiny plug into their quotes for the businesses that they run, which you remembered and maybe Googled straight afterwards? Yup, me again.

Magazines, TV shows, radio, or most websites rarely do features on a business unless it's:

- A paid-for advertorial.
- An article with celebrity involvement – Jamie Oliver, Ewan McGregor, Clare Baldwin
- An expose of the horrendous business practices that have ruined 1000s of lives

The media's job is to make content that their audience wants, meaning they carry on buying the magazine/watching the channel, so their advertisers can deliver to their target audience. So, offering them what their audience wants is the first step to getting coverage.

* **Be prepared** - Imagine, after a lifetime as a pub singer, getting an invite to sing at Wembley Stadium with Adele. You wouldn't just turn up, would you? At the very least you'd learn the words, maybe take some lessons, and ask exactly what it was she wanted.

What you wouldn't do is just rock up unprepared. Yet this is, essentially, what people do to journalists every day of the week. They send the same story idea to dozens of journalists on different publications/programs/websites, with little consideration of the kind of content they're looking for – or the needs of their audience.

The message is this: "I want you to help ME, by giving ME column inches or airtime, but I'm not prepared to put in the time to understand what YOU need." No wonder journalists can be grumpy.

If you want to give yourself the best possible chance of getting coverage in a magazine or newspaper (or on radio or TV), you should invest some time researching the places you're pitching to so you can get a sense of the kind of content they typically run.

* **Make it easy for them** – Media outlets have tight budgets for editorial content and anything that looks like a great feature for their

core audience that can be made easily and cost-effectively will look very appealing indeed. Plus, the boundaries between editorial and advertising are blurring, especially online, meaning that a smart business owner, who understands their audience can get some good coverage by giving the media what their (and your) customers want in a simple, good-value package.

You should be pitching ideas that tell your customer's stories and engage with others in the same arena. Your business's involvement is seemingly incidental, but somehow prominent in the story. For example, a few years ago, the sewing shop I owned (a completely different story) invited a magazine to come along and take part in a workshop we were running. The workshop helped local sewing enthusiasts learn how to work with a particularly difficult fabric – something that many of the magazine readers would identify with.

The magazine got a great feature about working with this fabric and our little shop got some amazing publicity about our friendly, effective, good-value workshops, including some lovely photos that showed what an inspiring place it was. We consequently saw a huge increase in customers, especially during the holiday season, from people who'd seen the article. Thinking laterally helps here.

Rather than just talking about your business, think about maybe an article on 'The challenges of setting up a small business". Or 'The joys of setting up a small business in the age of social media'. Picking up on the hot topics of the day can give your pitch an interesting angle too. It doesn't matter if your business is conventional, adding an unconventional or populist twist to the story will get it noticed.

You, the media and imposter syndrome

You may not be too surprised to hear that most people who feel like an imposter in their own business are women.

"I just got lucky"

"I'm a fraud, and everyone will find out soon enough"

"I don't belong here"

"I'm not good enough"

"I'm not an expert, really"

"No one will want to listen to me"

Sound familiar?

We all have feelings of doubt at some point but when all the things you've achieved are a result of your hard-won knowledge, enviable work ethic and preparation, and you still feel inadequate, you have a big, bad dose of imposter syndrome. You're succumbing to a persona (in your head, that is) of someone who you are not.

As business owners, we want to attract clients we love, and that means getting visible. Really visible. And yet, just the mention of being in the media sets imposter syndrome off in a stampede. It's the thought of being seen and heard by thousands of people that does it. And what about the journalists? They're going to wonder who the hell you are, aren't they? "No" is the answer to that. Let me explain.

There is so much demand for media now. All the print stuff, online, blogs, podcasts, 24-hour TV and radio. Just imagine how much content it takes to keep all these wheels spinning and journalists don't have the expertise to talk about everything. They rely on experts to fill in the blanks for them. By doing my research, I can write about anything, but only to a point. When it comes to the nitty gritty of the detail, I need help. I need your expertise. This is the same for all media platforms. If a journalist is writing about dieting, they'll need a nutritionist. Dog stories need a canine specialist. Instagram articles need a social media expert.

Why can't this expert be you? It can. Show them how good you are, and they'll be falling over themselves to use you.

But it takes courage to be seen – properly seen as who we are. And just like when we were kids trying to avoid doing our homework, we'll set out doing a ton of stuff that doesn't do anything for our visibility rather than focus on what will.

Conquering Imposter Syndrome is a process. It all starts with being aware when it's holding you back – that's probably your signal that it's the very thing you need to get over to be more visible and more successful. Ask yourself, if you could overcome this limiting belief, how would that change things for you?

Would you be hosting a workshop, leading a Facebook Group, collaborating with influencers, starting a blog, podcast or YouTube channel? Being interviewed on GMTV or Woman's Hour? Yep, thought so – but these are for later, right? When you have a moment.

No, that's not true, and Imposter syndrome is a limiting belief that cripples many. You are more than capable of being in the media and growing your business. Journalists are going to love you.

Julie Brown

Visibility and Media Coach

Scan or click on the above QR code to claim your bonus gifts and free resources from the featured authors! qrco.de/bcrTuK

Chapter 9

Helen Vandenberghe - Mentor To Rising Stars

The Power of Money
Step Up And Charge Your Worth

It was 6am on a grey, rainy Tuesday morning, as I heard my mum's key in the lock. She'd just finished a night shift as a cleaner in a local hotel - home in time to get us to school before she started her second job. I crept down the stairs to see her counting out her earrings and putting it into little brown envelopes. Two pounds towards the electricity bill, four pounds for the gas, a pound saving towards Christmas. She shuffled coins from one envelope to another, muttering to herself, and I could see her eyes were red with tears as she struggled to stretch the meagre budget.

As she kicked off her shoes, I noticed a massive hole in one of the soles. Her tights were soaked where she'd walked home in the rain. And it just broke my heart.

Up until that point, I'd been your typical self-absorbed teenager. I never knew money was that "tight". On birthdays, I always seemed to get the latest trendy toy or gadget. We were always fed, clothed, and cared for. Little did I know Mum was scrimping for months to afford such luxuries that were casually tossed aside when the novelty had worn off.

This woman, who was so full of love and kindness, was doing everything she could to support her family, but was always running at the edge. I knew that just a little extra income would make a massive difference to the entire household.

And that's where my entrepreneurial journey began.

I became obsessed with figuring out how I could earn some money for the family - I was too young for a part-time job and I started buying a trade magazine 'The Exchange & Mart', which was a wholesale directory and was full of "make money now" ideas.

My mum and I loved going to markets, craft fairs, and county shows, where people sold goods they'd made or bought at reasonable prices. So ,my first idea was to purchase some stock - what they used to call "fancy goods", and hire a stall at a market. But how was I going to pay for the stock, with my 50 pence per week pocket money?

I then realized that not only would this incur some upfront investment (which I didn't have), there was no guarantee that I would actually sell anything... but the person who was selling the pitches at the market was almost guaranteed to make some money- AND they got paid in advance!

I asked the caretaker at the local community hall if I could host a market there. He kindly let me reserve the space without a deposit until I got bookings.

And so, at the age of 14, I started my first business, renting out tables in a village hall for small business owners to sell their crafts and produce.

I put posters around the local villages and towns, saying we were looking for stall holders. Soon I had people wanting to sell everything from honey to houseplants, jewelry to jigsaws. Many of these were women who were doing this to make a little extra money on the side... just like me.

I loved hearing their stories of how they came up with their business idea, or how they created their produce or crafts.

On the day of the market, the whole family got involved. My brother helped me set up the tables in the hall. My sister and mum handed out leaflets to passersby, promising free cakes (which they'd made the night before) to all who attended, and my dad cycled round the village on his rickety bicycle with a megaphone shouting, "Come to The Jubilee Market".

We ended the day exhausted, excited and £150 better off. It was the most money I'd ever seen!

As I ran the market over the next two years, I learned many lessons (don't try to make 300 cups of tea with one domestic kettle, don't leave your naughty Labrador in the same room as all the cakes), but I also learned that I had a natural flair for marketing and business.

I could easily see where a business owner could make more money by, perhaps, packing a toy and a book together, or by displaying their products more attractively. Soon many of the stall holders were asking me for advice on how to layout their stands, or how to price their products.

Over two years, I was able to contribute over £14,000 to our family's income (in the 1980s) - which was frankly life-changing for us. And while I'm sure I drove my sister and brother mad with my hair-brained ideas ("Hey Sis, how about you dress up as a clown and stand outside?"), we bonded immensely over this period - particularly when my dad got a job abroad and was away for months at a time.

I could also see the pride the local mums took in offering their handmade jewelry, home-made cakes, or even the latest Aloe Vera range that they truly believed in. I could also see the difference the extra income made. Whether it was being able to afford to send their kids on a school trip, or being able to cover their bills with more ease, it made a big difference. I also noticed that almost all the female business owners had some way of giving back. Many of them donated a percentage of their profits to a charity, or donated unsold produce to a homeless shelter.

When women did well in their business, they did good for their community.

Finally, at the age of 16 I was ready to move on, and handed the market over to a local women's group who ran it for the next 20 years (damn, I wish I'd arranged a profit share)!

. . .

I was incredibly fortunate to have had such a positive experience with money and business at such a young age. And it set me on the path to becoming obsessed with empowering women to become financially independent through business.

Now, three decades later, I run a women's empowerment company where we help female coaches, consultants and experts to grow their business to six and seven figures.

As a company, we serve thousands of women around the world with our coaching and consulting programs, The Fully Booked Formula™, The Unleashed & Unlimited Mastermind™, and our flagship "Million Dollar Author" programs, where we teach business owners to write and launch a book that generates leads, enquiries and sales for their highest level services.

I have personally mentored hundreds of women, and I've noticed that many female entrepreneurs run into the same blocks when growing their business. In the next section, we'll dive into what could be putting a handbrake on your success, and how to have quantum leaps in your business right now!

Female Entrepreneurs and Money

I see so many incredible coaches, experts and consultants unconsciously setting their pricing based on fear, self-doubt or limiting beliefs they have around money instead of solid business strategy. When this happens, our money mindset can keep our prices (and our bank accounts) stuck and unnecessarily low, certainly smaller than the vision we have for ourselves and our biz. Why? Because our beliefs guide our actions. Just recognizing these blocks as the unfounded, limiting beliefs they are, can help you free yourself from their shackles and help you start charging what you're worth.

So what are some common money blocks? Below I will outline five that could be keeping you from charging way less than you deserve.

1. **My Clients Won't Pay That!** - This is often a story we tell ourselves to keep ourselves safe (and small).
2. **I've Got to Charge Less Than My Teacher/Mentor** - Your pricing should be based far more on the results you help your clients achieve.

3. **I Need to Discount To Win Business** - Most prospects are looking for the best value rather than just the cheapest price alone.
4. **Making Money is Hard** - It doesn't have to be.
5. **This Task is Easy/Fun For Me - It Seems Wrong To Charge For Something I Find So Easy.** - You're absolutely entitled to be well compensated for working to your strengths and in your zone of genius.

How do you communicate your value as a coach or expert?

First, focus on the results you achieve with your clients. Use the power of stories to show the true value of your services. Tell people what inspired you to do what you do, and share results of clients and testimonials in all your marketing.

Next, stop undercharging. Undercharging is one of the biggest ways women keep themselves small in business. You might think that charging lower fees lets you work with clients who really need your help but wouldn't be able to afford the fees you'd secretly like to be charging. But how would you feel if - because you were bringing in enough income working with clients who were paying you what you're really worth - you were able to help those unable to pay - completely free of charge? Pretty great, right? Undercharging is keeping you from that experience.

Finally, Lovingly Hold Your Boundaries. It reminds your clients that your expertise, time and attention are all valuable and to not squander them.

One of my clients, Jennie, was running a successful mastermind with 14 amazing clients, but she was exhausted and reaching burnout as she felt at the "beck and call" of her VIP clients who were texting and messaging her 24/7. We helped Jennie redesign her program, building her team, creating a curriculum that fully supported her clients' needs, including accountability pods, and setting clear boundaries. She was now finally able to take vacations without feeling she was letting her clients down, and also was able to scale, bringing in another 50 clients in 12 months, without doing more hours.

So Why Should You Attract Premium Clients?

Of course, you don't need to work exclusively with premium clients (unless, of course you want to), but experience tells me that premium high-paying clients will tend to be your best, most eager, and easiest to work with clients. These clients will also tend to get the best results.

Why? There seems to be a correlation between financial investment and personal investment. Clients who pay bigger fees to work with you can often be more committed to taking action and seeing a return on their investment.

Is It Ethical To Sell 'High-End' Services - Given The World Economy Right Now?

As I'm writing this, we're just coming out of a global pandemic and currently dealing with a very real war in the Ukraine. I hope by the time you read this, these situations will be resolved, but the truth is that at any one time, many countries will be facing difficulties (there are over 40 conflicts happening around the world right now). And yet, there will always be a premium end to in market. Also, the term "high-end" is relative. $15,000 may seem like a bargain to some people and a life's savings to others. It's much easier to reach your income goals at $3,000, $5,000 or $15,000 chunks. And when you have more, you are able to donate money, time or resources to causes you believe in.

My recommendation is to have a flagship premium program or service, alongside some more affordable options which require less of your time and focus.

No one is served if you shrink during tough times and feel guilty for making money when others are struggling. There are many ways you can serve the world, and allowing your business to thrive and grow will not only give you the resources to do more, but could be an inspiration for others.

Will People Really Pay That Much?

The short answer is yes. If you position, package and promote your offer the right way.

Lots of people assume that their current clients won't be interested in investing in extra time or resources. In fact the opposite is true.

No matter what field you're in, at least a small percentage of your potential clients are likely to be interested in working with you in a more in depth and/or intimate way; getting more support from you; and/or accessing additional content.

If you don't have a higher end offer, you are leaving (potentially heaps of) money on the table.

This is especially true if you're seen as a credible expert in your industry.

One of my clients, Linda Barbour, came to us charging less than $100 for her expert psychotherapy services. She has over 20 years of experience but felt invisible in her industry. Within weeks of working with us she had raised her rates more than 15 times, and was delighted to enroll 4 clients immediately.

And stop worrying about whether or not you're "affordable". Sure, we want our fees to be aligned to our ideal client, but when we become overly focused on affordability, we're making financial decisions for others. And that can totally backfire, even be seen as offensive to some of our potential or current clients. And I bet, like me, you'd hate for that to happen.

So, How Do You Get These Illusive Premium Clients Online?

First Build Credibility. When you position yourself as a credible expert, opportunities can quickly snowball. You're more likely to attract ideal clients and charge (and be paid!) a premium for your services. Instead of being just another face in the crowd, solid credibility can help you more easily become a trusted advisor and thought leader in your field. Here's some tips to get you started.

Get Visible

Create a strategy for showing up online. I love automated webinars where clients can find me night and day, but I also have a complete organic strategy for live events, which works amazingly well by tapping into other people's audiences. This is especially helpful if you have a small audience or limited email list.

Give Value

Create one CORE piece of valuable content that positions you as the expert. This could be a book, challenge, webinar, launch or video series. We helped our client, Mary Silver, to brand and launch her first book, achieving best-seller in six categories and creating the Impact Millions virtual conference - which reached thousands of potential clients around the world. She gave immense value to her audience and now is building a global brand from it.

Make Offers

The fastest way to enroll PREMIUM clients is to get them on the phone/Zoom/Skype and have a REAL conversation with them. All your marketing should encourage people to either consume your high-value content or book a call with you.

Are You Our Next Success Story?

If you KNOW you are ready to make more Impact and Income, I would love to gift you our Fully Booked Formula™ Blueprint and masterclass where you can discover how to get a consistent flow of pre-qualified premium potential clients booking into your calendar every week without constant blogging, expensive ads, or spending every minute of your day on social media, make sure you check out my gift and short video by scanning the QR code that is listed throughout this book!

Scan or click on the above QR code to claim your bonus gifts and free resources from the featured authors! qrco.de/bcrTuK

Chapter 10

Tanya Abdul Jalil

**Stories beyond fear sharing your story,
even when you're scared!**

"Everything you've ever wanted is on the other side of fear", said George Addasir.

What fears are holding you back, and why are you letting them have such power over you?

When it comes to sharing your personal story with your audience, fear is the most common reason I hear from client for not fully stepping into their brand story. And coming close after fear is its good friend, perfectionism.

The truth is, fear and perfectionism are holding you back from achieving your dreams because they stop you from being true to yourself.

Fear and perfectionism can lead to:

- Copying others, because they look like they have it all together

- Procrastinating and not taking action, because you can't decide where to start
- Hiding, or playing small because you're a people pleaser at heart and you don't want to let people down by changing who you are
- Wasting time creating content because you don't have a clear voice to share
- Not getting the sales you want, because your audience are getting mixed messages about who you are and what you do.

It's easy to look at your coaching idols and think they have it all together. *If only I just copy everything they do, I'll be just like them.* But you can't ever be the same as someone else. And you shouldn't want to be. If there was a line-up of coaches, who all taught the same thing... you don't want to be like every other coach in your industry, you want to stand out. You want to show your audience the things that make you relatable and approachable.

You want to share your story.

What's at the root of all that fear?

Fear is your brain's protection system. It pops up when you're about to do something scary, that could be dangerous, like jumping off a cliff. But sometimes it goes into overdrive, and things that make us even a bit uncomfortable, like public speaking, spark a sense of fear.

When it comes to sharing your story, fear often comes from not wanting to step out of line. We're conditioned from an early age to live up to the expectations that others put on us. People start telling our story before we're even born.

We're our grandparents' third grandchild; our parents' second daughter; the first boy in the family for 20 years; a new Saints supporter. We're going to grow up and follow the family traditions of holidays and the beach, and running the family business.

This storytelling continues as we grow up and forge our own identity. We become sporty or smart (or a lucky combination of both). We become serious or funny, are big dreamers, and potential change makers, or humble homebodies, that want a quiet life and three kids.

· · ·

All of these stories have the power to come true. And most of the time we don't argue. We get swept along with the tide of life and go through the motions of life without much thought or resistance.

Life was simpler growing up in the before the internet. You grew up, got a job, and did that job until you retired. You might change employers a few times, but stayed in the same profession for life. The smart girls had a choice of nursing or teaching. Less academic girls went into hairdressing, or retail. Same for the boys; law, medicine, or accounting for the clever (or wealthier) ones, and trades for those who didn't enjoy studying.

Growing up, we never knew that you could, and most likely would, change your entire career to something new. Modalities and careers like coaching, healing, mentoring may have existed in the 80s, but were far from our field of consciousness. We never could have imagined taking on professions that could see us sharing our skills and knowledge with literally anyone on the planet, via the internet.

What happens when you, your parents, your friends and colleagues have all grown up with these expectations... and you suddenly want to make a move to a new career? You get hit with a wall of fear. Fear of what other people will think of you. Fear of trying something new, and fear of not being good enough.

Negative self-talk starts to tell you all the reasons why you should keep playing small.

"If you leave, then you'll have wasted all that time and money spent studying. All those career accolades are down the drain. You'll never earn the same money or prestige. You'll miss the sick leave and holiday pay..."

It's a never ending list, and each and every one of those things stems from fear.

But remember... everything good that you want is on the other side of fear.

When we tell our stories of who we are, we're tapping into those stories of who we were told we'd be. And the stories that we told ourselves we'd be. Now, we're adding the next chapter to that story. We're doing something different. And scary. And ground breaking. And that thing that we're doing, that no one else in our family or friends has done, opens us up to all sorts of judgement, even, and especially from ourselves.

Storytelling matters

Story is the thread that connects us, from our ancestors to our children. We tell the stories of our families, our cultures, our people. These stories might be the big life lessons stories from our religion that teach us how to be good humans and how to treat each other. They may be small stories told when passing a familiar childhood hangout where you met your first love. These stories are remembered and retold because they are relatable and emotional.

When we tell stories in our business, it goes beyond facts and figures and creates an emotional connection that starts to build a relationship. Imagine for a second that two identical coaches have a new course. The first tells you that the course will help you make a thousand dollars a month. The second, knows you and your needs. They know what a difference that money would make in your life. They know if you'd spend the money on therapy sessions for your kids, paying off your mortgage and bills, or if you'd use the money to take your family on a month-long vacation each year. Which coach are you more likely to buy from? The one who tells your story like it's their own.

For coaches, healers, trainers and educators of all descriptions, you aren't selling a product you can boast about the features of. You're selling YOU. When your clients buy from you, they aren't buying just a course or coaching package. They're buying a chance to transform their lives in some way. When you tell your story with confidence, you're showing them how they can build the same confidence, and come through the experience transformed, just like you.

You can be the best coach, guide, leader or mentor on the planet, but if your audience doesn't know you exist, then they won't find you. Unless you're telling your story over and over again, sharing who you are, what you do and how you can help; then people won't be buying.

Finding our stories

Before we can go out into the world and share our stories and transform the lives of others, we need to be confident in ourselves. That self-belief, that our purpose on the planet is to do this life-changing work, needs to be embedded deep in our soul.

In order to find our stories, we need to find what makes us stand out from the crowd. Your audience is not looking for someone the same as everyone else. They want that special magic that only you can provide.

The central element of your stories is YOU.

What are the things that will make you stand out from the crowd?

What do you bring from your:

- Family
- Culture
- Country
- Relationships
- Family status
- Education
- Skills
- Knowledge
- Experiences

No one on earth has the same fabulous mixture of parts that you do. And this is what makes you special. These things are also the touch points that connect us to our clients. They make us real and relatable. When you bring yourself to the story, you can add in all those emotions and feelings and real transformation that you've experienced that help your clients see themselves in your story, too.

Never assume people understand how your brand can change their lives – tell them. Donald Miller

Tell a new story.

Our experiences are deeply shaped by our ancestors that came before us. The stories and beliefs that our grandparents were given by their parents shaped who they became. They then passed these beliefs and stories onto your parents, who ingrained them into you. Older generations who have seen us grow up and find our purpose can speak from fear. Not because they want to keep us down, but because it's all they've ever known.

Things like:

- Girls should always...
- Boys can...
- Good wives/husbands/children must...
- No one in our family has ever...

These are stories that we've all been told. But that doesn't make them true. There's always a counterpoint to each of these, and you can be that exception to the rule. Go out and change the stories your family tells about girls, boys, relationships, work, careers, families, and marriages. Reframe the stories you tell yourself and train the people around you to reframe their stories, too.

And finally, some thoughts on fear.

When it comes to trying new things, I'm a big fan of "do it scared". It's easy to make excuses for why we can't do something. But we only get one chance at this life, and time will pass regardless. You can either do the thing and possibly change your life, or you can stay small and not step out of your comfort zone.

Literally, no one on earth will judge you, or care if you don't step up and share your story. But there are costs if you don't. There's the always wondering "what if". There are the people out there struggling that need your help. There are the people who love you and who are cheering you on, who are watching you and want you to reach your full potential.

Who are you letting down by not stepping up?

It's ok to do something that's never been done before.

It's ok to be exactly who you are in this moment, without knowing all the answers, but knowing enough to take the next step forward.

"Those who tell the stories rule the world." - Hopi American Indian proverb

Thrive and Prosper

Scan or click on the above QR code to claim your bonus gifts and free resources from the featured authors! qrco.de/bcrTuK

Chapter 11

Laura Lee Kenny

WHEN YOU ARE STUCK IN THE DRAMA TRIANGLE

How do you get out?

Ring, ring, the phone was ringing. "Hello honey, how are you?" said a male voice from the other end of the phone.

"Did you get lost?" he chuckled.

"Kind of," came with a sobbing voice and, "I can't figure out how to get home. "Can you help... me... figure this out...," she said slowly through quiet whimpers.

"You're joking, right?" Were the words that came through the phone.

"Did you try using the GPS?" Was Ed's first suggestion.

"Yes, I did. I can't figure out how to get across the river. Both bridges are closed. Repairs on one and completely closed off, as there is a terrible accident on the other. Everything is backed up for over 60 minutes. They announced it on the radio." I slowly explained my dilemma. (Traffic jams are not a common situation in a Maritime city of only 100,000 people.)

. . .

"Well, just drive around until you get your bearings," was my loving hubby's suggestion.

"No, I can't think straight. I should not be driving." Came from a cranky, exhausted voice. "I just wanted to let you know I was still alive, and I'll get home when I can. I'll walk to a restaurant and get some water and a cup of tea. I'll rest for a while and see if that helps. I'll call later," I said quietly.

"OK, let me know in a bit. See you later, bye" were Ed's parting words in a soothing voice.

It was hard to believe that I was so confused. I just could not figure things out. Being exhausted, I understood. We have had more than our share of disasters lately. Our family lost 2 forty-year-old nieces within months. One from a rare type of cancer and the other from a seizure and then a stroke. One of my brothers was the next to pass away at age 57, MY mom at age 80, a brother-in-law at age 70, and a sister at age 63. Plus, there we a handful of life-threatening health issues with several immediate family members. A Lot of heart issues to deal with. There is a saying that things come in threes. Well, it was multiples of threes. Rest in peace Jennifer, Peggy, Kevin, Jean, Danny, Ellen.

Then we lost our happy place, our adorable summer cottage, where we spent 7 glorious months of the year. We put a tremendous amount of money into raising the cottage and adding huge decks to protect our investment in case of a flood. We felt we were safe. It was where we planned to retire and spend a few winter months in a warmer climate. Gone on the last day during a historic flood with tornado-type winds. Gone in 15 minutes, when there was no water inside of the cottage. And the insurance would not pay for anything.

Life was really challenging us. During the clean-up period, I had been knocked on the head and collapsed on my butt on the ground twice, and physically got hurt a total of 4 times. I even had to go to the emergency department, 3 times because of the accidents. My husband joked that soon the police were going to come knocking at the door to check for spousal abuse. I might have been suffering from a concussion that was making me even more clumsy. I wasn't running on all cylinders, that was for sure. I needed new spark plugs, or at least a tune-up. As my mentor, with Eden energy medicine, would explain, I was not balanced. Apparently, I needed to work on myself, not the world.

Oh, the drama triangle, did I ever have it bad. The poor me, victim; life isn't fair. I'm a good person, so how could this happen to me? I definitely never wished for anything like this to ever happen. How can they say you get what you wish for or what you think about? Oh my God. That's crazy. One minute, I felt I was on top of the world. Life was fun and enjoyable, then disaster strikes and strikes and strikes! I moved from victim (poor me) to persecutor (blames everyone else) to rescuer (I'll help you) in no apparent rhythm.

How do I change my circumstances? I don't want to live this type of life! I was a very happy, bubbly person who always saw the glass half full. Full of rainbows and dreams of improving my life and the people around me. My life had to change, and I needed help. I didn't want to stay in this rut any longer. Three years was way too long of a sentence of just existing, certainly not living an abundant life.

All the training I had wasn't enough on my own. And I knew that the average healthy person would need help to deal with 2 or more severe life changes within a year, let alone double digits events. I wasn't sure how, but what I did know, it wasn't going to be from a bottle of pills from the doctor. So off I went in search of help and guidance for a happy life.

We often hear that the older we get, the less likely we are to change. But change we must in order to evolve and thrive. You either get that bitter or you get better. It' is that simple. You either deal with the hand you have been dealt and allow it to make you a better person, or you allow it to tear you down. The choice does not belong to fate; it belongs to you.

Repetitive complaining will attract things for you to complain about.
Repetitive gratitude will attract things for you to be thankful about.

I was given the nickname of Medicine Woman when I was in my early twenties because of my alternative choices for modern medicine. It was interesting that I had started my education in Eden energy Medicine methods in April 2018. Donna's teachings helped me a lot in dealing with stress and balance. But when I was knocked down by being hit on the head with steel beams, I needed physical help from other practitioners. I was so out of balance, and I felt like I was running on a treadmill, not getting anywhere, but exhausted.

My guardians angels were Eva and Sue to the rescue. And it took some time and a lot of practice for me to start feeling like my old self and staying in the happy flow. Techniques I continue to practice and do for myself every day because I deserve the best. We all do. It is like putting the oxygen mask on yourself first, before helping others. We can't give from an empty cup.

So, I started with awareness. Got back into practicing gratitude and appreciation for what I still had. One thing that helped me smile for a few minutes was looking at baby pictures or videos, especially if you could see or hear them laughing. My heart would swell up with joy and gratitude. I didn't need to know the babies, as they represented hope to me. For some people, it could be animal videos that give them joy. Thank you, Facebook for these postings.

You know that the Heart Math Institute, in the US, tells us the 4 top healing words. And how we are feeling when stating these words is the most important part of the exercise.

1. Appreciation for anything and anyone.
2. Gratitude for anything and anyone.
3. Care for anything and anyone.
4. Compassion for anything and anyone.

To make these words even more effective, lightly touch your heart or put your hands in a prayer position in front of your heart, breathing in and out very slowly for 4 seconds, holding your breath for 4 seconds, and releasing for 4 seconds. Remember that it can take three days to have a healing experience for some people. This makes great sense to me.

Starting with the feelings of appreciation and gratitude was a mindset shift for me. Which was so easy when I decided to get out of self-pity, and what I felt was the unfairness of the people in the companies that let me down. I was reacting to life situations. There were better ways to deal with grief and loss.

. . .

We're told that we grow personally during times of turmoil; how we handle ourselves during and after. Some of us are masters by now! As long as we live, there will be more times for us to practice gratitude, look forward, not back, set ourselves up to win.

Another one of my amazing mentors made sense of the Drama Triangle and how to help others to heal and get out of the Drama Triangles. This was an enormous lesson for me. I chuckle to myself when I listen to other people talk about their life now. It is interesting how quickly we can see what others are doing and saying.

I have been taught that we empower and guide, not just tell others the answers or directions. We are all here to help and guide one another in healing and thriving.

There is a reason some people say that we must put our big girl panties on and get on with life. And yes, some might even call them granny panties.

Here are five things you might want to quit right now:

1. Trying to please everyone
2. Fearing change
3. Living in the past
4. Putting yourself down
5. Overthinking

Decisions, we can think about things, turnover in our minds a million times playing impossible scenarios, but really when it comes down to it, you have to go with your heart and gut feelings. Get on and move forward. Maybe things will go well, maybe they'll turn out poorly. Every decision brings with it some good, some bad, some lessons, and some luck.

The only thing that's for sure is that indecision steals many years from many people who wind up wishing they just had the courage to leap. We are told to leap, and the net will appear. That's what I choose to do. It was a shame that I wasted a few years not making the decision to put myself first for the healing. Everyone in my family benefited from me being healthy.

If you could be the director, producer, and shining star in your own blockbuster movie, would you, do it? I can help you write your own script.

It's one of my favorite abundance tools to change old limiting beliefs and unleash your potential.

What will it cost to stay where you are?

Here's the cold, hard truth.

No one can help you unless you are willing to help yourself. You even have all the answers inside of you.

So why would you need me for your coach?

When you're inside the problem, it is really hard to see the way out. Let me help you with that. Let me help you find the key to unlock the answers you hold inside you.

You just need direction and guidance. So, save yourself some time, which we never have enough of, and live the best life you can. Hire yourself some HELP. That is what coaches love to do. Together, we can level up your life to have quantum leaps. Give yourself permission to choose self-love first. Start the healing.

So, if you want to make a quantum shift, go to the QR code that is shown on the following page and claim your FREE relaxation recording and begin saying Yes to you and your new Abundant life.

Many blessings and gratitude to all. Thank you for reading.

Have a Great Day and a Better Tomorrow.

Laura Lee

Scan or click on the above QR code to claim your bonus gifts and free resources from the featured authors! qrco.de/bcrTuK

Chapter 12

Tara E. McGillicuddy

Shift Your Energy, Shift Your Life

One thing I have often been told by people over the years is that they liked my energy. When I was younger, I hadn't yet been trained to work with energy and really hadn't given it much thought. When I used to attend ADHD conferences and support my colleagues by attending their sessions, I was told it was great to have me and my energy there. When I did an internship years ago as I was finishing up and saying goodbye, I was told they would miss me and my energy. This became a common theme, and it wasn't until years later that I began to understand what it truly meant and the impact I have on people's lives by helping them shift their energy.

As human beings, we all have the ability to affect and shift energy. Being able to help shift somebody's energy in a positive way is a blessing and maybe even a gift. With that being said, it's also important to understand that we are all capable of shifting energy in negative ways as well. It's essential that we are mindful of both the negative and positive effects our words, thoughts, and actions have on ourselves, other people, and the world.

Gratitude

One of the best ways to positively shift the energy is to practice gratitude. Many people have gratitude lists and gratitude journals, and those can be a great start to practice gratitude. Practicing gratitude, however, goes beyond just thinking or writing about gratitude. Practicing gratitude is about being in the feeling and energy of gratitude. It's essential that we go beyond just thinking about what we are grateful for, and that we BE in **gratitude.**

If you are somebody who has a gratitude journal or makes gratitude lists and it's something you benefit from, by all means keep up with them. We don't need them to be in the energy or feeling of gratitude, though. Being in gratitude is as simple as taking a few moments to think of something or somebody you are grateful for then tap into that feeling and energy of gratitude.

Gratitude is something that can be practiced anywhere, at just about any time. Some people find it helpful to practice gratitude as part of a routine or ritual at the same time or times every day. One program I offer as a coach is a productivity group. I end each session by having the group members practice gratitude during the last few moments of the session. Some people practice gratitude first thing when they wake up or last thing before they go to sleep.

One of the most important and effective times to practice gratitude is when we are in a stressful situation. It can be challenging to transition to the energy of gratitude when we are in a stressful overwhelming, situation. Having what I call a "Go to Gratitude List" is very helpful. This is a short list of 1-5 things you are grateful for. The list can be in your head or it can be written down. When you are stressed, upset, or overwhelmed choose something from your "Go to Gratitude List" and tap into the energy and feeling of gratitude for a few moments.

When we go through stressful and negative situations, it is important to process the feelings and emotions associated with the situations. The energy and feeling of gratitude does not need to be connected or associated with every event or situation. Back in 2010, my best friend Pauline was dying from cancer and I went out to visit her to say goodbye. While I was there, I spent time with her family members, including her husband Joe. Joe and I took a ride together in his car and I expected him to break down or vent to me about the pain he was going through. He didn't do that, though. Instead, he told me how grateful he was for all the help and support people gave the family through Pauline's illness. I was amazed that somebody going through what he was going through could do that. Not all of us can do what Joe was able to, but we are all able to shift into the feeling and energy of gratitude.

Gratitude Affirmations and Questions:

- I am grateful for _____.
- How did I become grateful for _____?
- What would it take to become grateful for _____?

Practice saying or writing the questions or affirmation above and fill in the blank with something you are grateful for or something you would like to become grateful for. Start out with all three and see which one feels best for you and your specific situation. Test out how many times to say or write the affirmation or question. Try closing your eyes and see if a number comes to mind. Go with the first number that comes to mind.

Forgiveness

The act of forgiveness can make a huge impact in shifting energy in a positive direction. Forgiveness is less about the people who hurt or wronged and more about the person who was hurt or wronged. Forgiveness does not mean the forgiver condones or makes excuses for the person being forgiven, it is about healing. Forgiveness can be challenging and may not come easy, but it's very rewarding when we forgive. For some of us, it's easier to forgive other people than it is to forgive ourselves. Self-Forgiveness is extremely powerful and healing.

While forgiveness helps to positively shift our energy, holding on to feelings of anger, hurt and resentment stagnates our energy and even brings it down. There are some situations when we can forgive right away and some that take more time. Sometimes we need to go outside of ourselves for help and support with forgiveness. Consider types of things like working with a mental health professional, working with an energy healer, and reading a book about forgiveness. Simple putting out the intention that would like to forgive is a step in the right direction.

Forgiveness affirmations and questions:

- I forgive myself.
- How did I forgive myself?
- What would it take to forgive myself?
- I forgive myself for _____?
- How did I forgive myself for _____?
- What would it take to forgive myself for _____?
- I forgive (name of person).
- How did I forgive (name of person)?
- What would it take to forgive (name of person)?
- I forgive (name of person) for _____?
- How did I forgive (name of person) for _____?
- What would it take to forgive (name of person) for _____?

Practice saying or writing the questions or affirmations above and fill in the blank with what it is you would like to forgive yourself, or somebody else for. In some situations, it makes sense to simply forgive a person. Other situations, it make sense to forgive a person for something specific. Start out with all three and see which one feels best for you and your specific situation. Test out how many times to say or write the affirmation or question. Try closing your eyes and see if a number comes to mind. Go with the first number that comes to mind.

The Power of Words

Spoken words and written words are extremely powerful when it comes to shifting energy. When the written and spoken words are combined, the power of the words are intensified. It is extremely important that we be very mindful of both the words we put out and the words we allow into our own life and our energy fields. We have the power and the ability to choose both what we allow in and what we put out there.

Boundaries are essential when it comes to media like the news, tv shows, movies and social media. It's time to begin questioning whether we are being informed and entertained or if we are being hurt and abused. Each of us differs from what we can tolerate and how it affects our energy. Pay close attention to how you feel and act after watching, reading, or listening to the different types of media. Try reducing or even eliminating different type of media and then pay attention to your energy. Even if we can't control what may be happening in the world, we have the power and ability to control the words we allow into our lives through the media.

The words of people we interact with in our everyday lives also have a huge impact on energy. Communication is a 2 (or more) way street. We can shift the energy of a conversation by responding instead of reacting. We can also choose carefully and use more positive words. It's also important that we have effective boundaries with people. Sometimes there are just some people who are negative and even abusive, no matter how we communicate with them. Reducing the amount of time or cutting them out of our lives maybe be the best solution.

The words we think, say, and write are very powerful. Everyday words like "can't", "should", "need", and "have to", negatively impact our energy. Replacing them with words like "will", "could", "like", creates more positive energy. Being more affirmative with our words shifts the energy to be more positive. Speaking with kindness and grace also adds more positive energy. Refraining from gossip, or what my friend Scott calls "Stink Talk" decreases negative energy.

Powerful Words Affirmation and Questions

- I communicate with kindness and grace.
- How did I start communicating with kindness and grace?
- What would it take to communicate with kindness and grace?
- I think healthy and positive thoughts.
- How did I start thinking healthy and positive thoughts?
- What would it take think healthy and positive thoughts?

Practice saying or writing the questions or affirmations above. Start out with all three and see which one feels best for you and your specific situation. Test out how many times to say or write the affirmation or question. Try closing your eyes and see if a number comes to mind. Go with the first number that comes to mind.

Scan or click on the above QR code to claim your bonus gifts and free resources from the featured authors! qrco.de/bcrTuK

Chapter 13

Christine Franklyn

The Secret to Getting Optimized for Success

Have you been hoping to find the physical and mental energy that will propel you to do everything you've always dreamed of?

Here's the harsh truth: striving for success the conventional way can cost you your life.

Most people will beat around the bush and sugar-coat it. Not me. Do you know why I take the straightforward approach? The reason is that I wish someone had used that approach with me. I managed to figure out the formula for getting out from under my high-pressure lifestyle so I could really thrive, but that was after many missteps along the way. Some people aren't that lucky. Their chronic stress and lack of attention to their health and well-being is not only holding them back, but it has also snowballed and is manifesting in a serious, sometimes fatal, illness.

The good news is that there's a way to achieve your goals without hurting yourself in the process.

The Journey that Felt Like a Thousand Miles

I have been told that I'm a born leader and everyone always knew they could count on me to get the job done. Sounds great, doesn't it?

No way! I used to be the poster-child for over-achieving and people-pleasing. Who do you think ended up the least pleased and burned out? You guessed it - yours truly!

My ever-on-the-go lifestyle left me with terribly low energy and was a recipe for disaster. Worse yet, my brain fog made me paranoid that I would forget something important. My brilliant solution at the time was to keep turning over my to-do list in my mind - a list that seemed to be as long as the Great Wall of China. I was so stressed out that not only was my energy zapped but also the flesh of my bones, like some super-charged vacuum, was depleting me of everything. My shoes were literally falling off my feet.

My nerves were on edge, my chest was always tight, and my head was often pounding. As for a personal life, what was that? I'm surprised my husband still recognized me.

If you can relate to any of this, it's time to turn it around, my friend.

The Solution No One is Talking About

A system of non-negotiable principles is the foundation of confident, successful people who show up as the best version of themselves in every area of their lives.

I'm not referring to core values, and I'm not talking about a set of activities, practices, or routines to be done daily. These non-negotiable principles are the bedrock that ensures any individual consistently puts himself or herself first. The actual principles vary from person to person, but each one sets up the way high achievers will move through life - powerfully, joyfully and vibrantly rather than weighed down by daily pressures.

The process of applying these self-awareness and self-improvement principles is not a quick fix and isn't perfected overnight, but you can get started right away. Here are some of the non-negotiable principles that are second nature to successful people:

Obligations will be made to fit the 80/20 rule

On any given day, the ratio of what I want to do vs what I feel I should do will be 80/20. Numerous little frustrations tend to stockpile and leave us feeling dissatisfied with our lives and deplete our energy. Get clear on what lights you up. If you've been avoiding specific tasks, your procrastination is a good sign that these tasks aren't aligned with you. Examine whether completing them will be the best use of your time or whether it may be a good idea to have them handled in some other way.

Are you feeling over-committed and overwhelmed? Then it's probably time to set some boundaries. Assess whether you can set realistic deadlines that can give you more breathing room. You may need to initiate some tricky conversations with demanding individuals, but it will be worth it in the long run. You are the leader of your life. No one else.

Tuning in is second only to breathing

No one wants to live a life of restriction. Feeling compelled to work in a certain way or eat according to a specific cookie-cutter meal plan or do workouts we don't like, none of this is any fun. Each one of us is uniquely designed with our own preferences and ways of doing things. That's why we each can make a mark on the world that no one else can. Celebrate that!

A lot has been written about the importance of meditation and mindfulness, and it's all totally valid. However, listening to your heart, body and spirit is not meant to be a once-a-day practice. Your body is sending you signals all day long and your spirit tells you when something just doesn't feel right. Stop and pay attention throughout the day.

Just as we are often told about the effectiveness of getting into a millionaire mindset, a similar approach is needed if you intend to nourish yourself to perform at your peak. The first step is committing to being self-aware before and after taking any action or making a decision, as well as being fully present in your experiences to assess what feels right and what doesn't. The aim is to be constantly learning about yourself so you make the choices that are aligned with you.

Honor what brings me joy

The freedom to say a wholehearted YES to whatever speaks to your soul is sure to bring you joy. Joyful living is not to be reserved solely for vacations or retirement; it's meant to be an everyday part of life and it makes us more resilient so we overcome challenges more easily. We all know that change is inevitable. Fortunately, joy does not rely on temporary external circumstances in the way that happiness does. It is a deep-seated feeling that makes us mentally strong and resilient.

The capacity to savor simple experiences and remain positive, even in difficult times, depends on how well an individual prioritizes joy filled activities. Don't put off the things you wish you had the energy or time to do. Take care of yourself and prioritize your well-being so you can bring those items on your "someday" list forward to today.

The 3 Pillars of my Power Up Formula

Life is not a dress rehearsal. Since we pass this way only once, why not get revved up to make the most of every worthwhile opportunity?

1. **Alignment-** High achievers tend to set up lofty expectations for themselves. The first step is to unravel how and why these self-imposed pressures emerged. My clients examine what they need and want out of life and then assess whether they are in alignment with their deepest desires. They get used to replacing adherence to misaligned obligations by giving themselves some grace and celebrating the little victories when things aren't going as planned. Calibrating your life doesn't happen overnight, but it's a muscle leaders can build step by step.

2. **High-Powered Energy-** Have you ever admired someone who seems energetic almost all the time? Leaders who work with me start to think like an expert energy strategist. In their business or career and their private life, they learn to carefully consider whether the choices they make are energy-depleting or energy-boosting. The reality is that low energy equals lost opportunities. If leaders want to have renewed vitality every day, it is essential for them to design their boundaries and personal habits as if they're skilled architects. They start to build into their daily schedule time to recharge their batteries. Before they know it, they feel stronger and more centered. Their brains are sharper so they can make better decisions. Best of all, they get a pep in their step and improved mental clarity and focus that helps them

get more done with ease. This frees up time to do more of what they love.

3. **Time Freedom**- There is no way to increase the number of hours in a day, no matter how badly many people would love to wave a magic wand to achieve this. The third pillar of my Power Up Formula is all about identifying and implementing systems and the right support to help clients take control of their time. They see that it really is possible to have the freedom to choose how and where they want to spend their days. It is an amazing feeling to no longer have to put out fires or be compelled to do things they dislike. Time spent engaged in meaningful activities, moving the needle where it matters, is priceless.

My client Rodney, who runs two businesses, wanted more energy and a healthier lifestyle. After working with me, he gained not only increased energy but also mental clarity and learned how to listen to his body.

"This is a sustainable practice for the rest of my life that helps me tune into what feels right. It's not about how to discipline myself. It's about what feels good in my body and that's way more sustainable for me moving forward."

It may sound counterintuitive, yet it really is possible to make positive changes without relying on our limited supply of self-discipline and willpower. It's an approach that works.

Mary Silver MSW

Scan or click on the above QR code to claim your bonus gifts and free
resources from the featured authors! qrco.de/bcrTuK

Chapter 14

Lisa Lorna Blair

It's your time to SHINE online!

I love holiday time – going on vacation! Who agrees? That feeling of booking the flights, selecting the accommodation, planning the itinerary, the day trips, checking the weather and the places to dine out, tourist attractions to visit. It's simply the best!

And when faced with a worldwide lockdown that brought international travel to a screeching halt, we all discovered a whole new appreciation for the ability to take adventures. Am I right???

Here's the thing!

When we go on a trip, we pack the clothing to suit the climate. We also add in the accessories we need – be it for a beach holiday, a ski trip, a hiking adventure or a mountain escape. What we do NOT do is pack every single item from our entire wardrobe, right? We pick and choose what we NEED. We don't bring ALL the baggage that we have accumulated over many years, like that old bowling t-shirt from a decade ago that holds sentimental value, the costume from last Halloween, or the bikini you wore in your 20s that you are determined to "get back into" before next summer!

· · ·

No! We are selective. We may fold and unfold, roll and then pack or re-pack several times, take things out, put things in. Then, as the deadline draws near to head to the airport or train station, we finalize what we are taking with us. (And even then, if you are like me, you still end up packing way more than you need!!)

The best trips away are amplified by our ability to bring with us only what we NEED for the destination we are heading to and for the amount of time we will spend there. When we get that right, the rest of it comes with ease and flow!

So, why is that when we start stepping into the role of mentor, coach or trainer, we drag all our old "baggage" with us there? We allow it to be a distraction to our ability to shine and enjoy success in the online space!

All those crazy things from decades past seem to come along for the ride. Or worse still, completely stop us in our tracks from saying YES to incredible opportunities – be it in business, coaching containers, or masterminds.

Imposter syndrome is a BIG one for nearly every person I know when they first start their online journey, be it as a coach, author, healer or speaker. "Who will want to hear what I have to say?" and "What value can I possibly share?" are common types of questions.

Procrastination, limiting beliefs, anxiety, doubt, self-worth. ALL of these are the "baggage" that comes with us. We hold ourselves back from truly shining our light and being the beautiful, bright, authentic beings that we are, because we are still holding on to the BS from the past! (Note: BS stands for "belief systems" but you may have another word you choose to use *wink*)

These ridiculous old stories get in the way. They create blocks and bumps in the road on our journey. But they do NOT have to come with us for every vacation or adventure!

We can allow them to weigh us down and come with us in the suitcase. Or we can see them for what they are, acknowledge their existence, THANK them (with gratitude) for the role they've played in keeping us safe. Then politely and firmly ask them to get out at the next stop and move on!! Their role is complete.

. . .

Owning my truth, living my fully expressed and authentic life, didn't happen overnight. My coaching, mentoring and support skills were latent for more years than I care to admit as I allowed the hurts, the pain, the betrayals, the perceived failures and limiting beliefs from the past to drive the bus.

I never went to therapy, but I did dive in and begin the healing journey with my mindset and personal development. I read the books; I took the courses and attended the seminars. I even tried network marketing and gained some self belief there, but soon discovered that my "up–line" were only keen to help me grow if I was helping their wallet to grow! Otherwise, you were quickly forgotten.

In 2019, I saw an opportunity to step fully into the online space and a whole new era of doing business, with ease and flow. When I saw just how many of my objections were overcome and I met the conscious entrepreneurs who were creating massive change and beautiful alignment, I felt the PULL. I already knew my best possible investment was ME and my own growth and so it was with that I began my deep dive into our beautiful self-paced Academy. Taking that step and saying YES to me opened the doors.

I realized I finally held Pandora's Box in my hands. And there was no turning back!

The incredible blend of online business strategy training and step-by-step business mentoring, right alongside the mindset, embodiment and personal growth components with some of the most inspirational soul-driven coaches and speakers on the planet, all blew my mind. And I knew, without a doubt, after years and years of searching, that I had found the formula to success.

Yes, I have Law of Attraction coaching, money mindset, nutrition coaching, NLP, Gratitude mentoring and so much more under my belt. And yes, there's also a bunch of incomplete courses and coaching programs that I signed up for and are still sitting in my inbox unopened (please tell me I am not the only one??!)

I had tools from years gone by, but I wasn't getting results. The skill set suite was incomplete. I had missed the vital first steps – the power and magic of the INNER WORK. So I set about changing those beliefs, kicking them to the curb, uncovering the blocks and moving them out of the way. FOREVER!

All while being part of an epic community of beautiful heart-centered and high vibe souls, transformational coaches, energy healers, as well as "tradies", network marketers, stay at home mums, light workers, traditional business owners and more!

We don't SELL; we ATTRACT. We don't "flog products" or cold call. We don't even sell to family and friends or insist they buy stuff. Instead, we simply introduce you to our monthly Academy membership and if it aligns with where you want to go, the financial and life goals you want to achieve, you jump in and try it for 14 days.

After checking it out, you will just KNOW whether this is the right fit for you.

Where you take it next is entirely up to you.

The steps are so simple and so joyous. Just dive in and start the Discovery Process, explore your perfect day, write it into existence, set your intention and goals and within a few steps you will just KNOW where you want to go and who you want to be. Forget the old network marketing model of "once size fits all" and doing it all the same as everyone else. Discovering your own personal brand, your own truth and authentic flow will allow you to see where you want to go and how you want to show up in the world with your value and your own unique gifts.

Why be like everyone else? You were divinely made and created to be unique. No other person on the planet is exactly like you.

For me – The Manifestation Muse – my focus is on the Law of Attraction, creating abundance and ease and flow in your life. Living from a space of "Gratitude being my attitude" and cutting through the noise on social media with positivity, joy, hope and authenticity.

And WOW, getting paid REALLY WELL to do so along the way!

My life's purpose and great joy now is supporting others to do the same, to unlock their own unique gifts and find their voice.

- Building relationships with amazing, heart-centered souls from all over the globe.

- Impacting lives and creating change.
- Having daily conversations and connections.
- Building wealth but also creating freedom, a more sustainable planet and placing health and wellness as a high value.

For me, the thriving survivor of life-saving open heart surgery, abundant health, will always be a high value!

Since diving into our Academy and building a personal brand online, everything in my life has changed. And it changes for everyone who dedicates their time to it!

We even have a mantra that we love to share: "The more fun we have, the more money we make!" because fun and celebrations are a big part of what we do.

When I unpacked the baggage, deleted the scarcity codes from my DNA, and embraced what is TRULY possible for every single one of us, the shifts began! And they continue to unfold.

Here's what has already happened in just three short years:

1. I retired myself from a corporate role after one year
2. Replaced my corporate salary and now have a six-figure business that is location-free
3. Have attracted my own tribe of like-minded high vibe souls that I am mentoring and empowering, from all over the world – Australia, The United States, the United Kingdom, Canada and more! (And there's always room for others!)
4. Paid off two credit cards, two mortgages and a vehicle
5. Manifested our incredible dream acreage property where we wake every morning to birdsong, surrounded by trees, nature and abundant life
6. Underwent life-saving open heart surgery to replace an aortic valve (and still earned income while I was offline, thanks to the automation of my business!)
7. Studied Law of Attraction coaching, Working with Angels training, THETA healing, NLP coaching, Nutrition and

wellness coaching, social media marketing, and personal branding

8. Created "The Manifestation Muse" community on Facebook, where I share gratitude and money manifesting workshops, deliver free content and value to support people to truly shine on their spiritual journey and growth

9. Recorded an abundance meditation coded with prosperity, THETA healing, and combined it with music created by my talented husband! * This short and powerful meditation has now been downloaded all over the world! (And yes, it's my FREE gift for you too)

10. Became a best-selling author

Every week our global tribe gathers on our Huddle and celebrates each and every "win" – be it big or small, personal, business or health related. As I keep saying, celebration is how we like to roll! The more we celebrate, the more it manifests for others.

In conclusion, please pay heed to my words of truth and wisdom...

Becoming a financially free female, a conscious wellness advocate, and Freedompreneur, living, thriving and shining my light, did NOT happen overnight. There's no such thing as "get rich quick". We all know this.

But... by unpacking the baggage, leaving it behind, de-cluttering my life from the elements that no longer serve a purpose or bring me joy and also by being willing to say YES to me, to learn and be coachable - all of this - unlocked the door to a truly rewarding, uplifting and vibrant life.

And now my mission is to support YOU, to create it in your way, too. I'm here to help you pack all the right clothes, accessories and tools for your own unique trip. To coach, mentor and inspire you to SHINE.

Here's what I remind myself every day and I want YOU to use this saying too:

"I deserve, I allow, I receive"

Yes, my friend, YOU are your own best INVESTMENT!! You have everything within you for greatness, you just need to unpack the unwanted baggage first!!

Support is within reach. Please ask and receive!

Scan or click on the above QR code to claim your bonus gifts and free resources from the featured authors! qrco.de/bcrTuK

Chapter 15

Dr. Allen Darbonne

Transforming Your Mind!

For A Passionate Deeper Soulmate Relationship

The #1 Most Important Step to Deeper Soulmating And Having Passionate, Joyful, Secure Love

> "I've learned that people will forget what you said, people will forget what you did, but people will never forget how you made them feel."
> Maya Angelou

Lovers and potential mates don't usually leave or stray because of how they feel about you. They leave or stray because of how they feel about themselves when they are around you. – Dr. Allen Darbonne

Let's You and I Connect

My inner guidance is that I need to start off this chapter by sharing with you my deepest sense of truth, my why for being on this planet, for taking my next breath.

I live for one thing, to express my spirit and my love, and to help others out of suffering and into spirit and love and happiness.

For 56 years, individuals in relationships, or who are wanting to be in amazing relationships, have hired me to help them create Passionate, Secure and Joyful soulmate love.

At the same time I know, from experience, how much this helps their children (over 1 million of which will suffer the effects of divorce this year) to go from helplessly suffering insecurities from having unhappy parents, to deep inner security and joyful thriving, and to becoming more generous and loving citizens on the planet.

This is my mission, my talent and my gift.

If you're reading this book, I treasure you, and I treasure your time. I would like to honor you by giving you some reasons it might be worthwhile to spend some time with me and read this chapter. First, I am 85 years old and have a s***- load of experience. I have had more time than almost any of you to make almost every mistake in the relationship book. And thanks to my parents, to learn and teach from my mistakes. I am eternally grateful to the incredible women who have allowed me to be in a relationship with them and to teach me things I needed to learn from them. I am also deeply sorrowed to realize that my learning process often caused unintentional pain to my partners in this process. I truly ask for their forgiveness for my errors and my learning curve.

Second, I have spent the last 50 plus years observing, studying, researching, and teaching about love relationships in many countries around the world. I have, and continue to work with relationship issues for CEOs of massive worldwide corporations and companies, professional athletes, members of the government, judges, lawyers, well-known actors, award-winning musicians and writers, prostitutes, criminals, professors, students, husbands, wives, children, lonely singles longing for love, and many other amazing individuals. I know and respect the nuances of different cultures and races, and I'm deeply touched by the genetic and spiritual similarity we all carry as humans. From what I have directly witnessed, it is easy for me to see that we are all brothers and sisters and cousins, part of a diversified line emanating from the same place and the same source generated many, many, many years ago.

I am professionally trained and experienced as a Relationship Psychologist, an Applied Brain Scientist, a Spiritual Teacher and Energy

Healer and a Leadership Coach and I bring all of these to serving others. At the same time, I am always in beginners' mind, and always aware that I am just like you, my brothers and sisters, a seeker and manifester in service on this amazing planet of ours. A little more experienced than some, a little less than others.

I have led summits and gatherings that included experts and participants from almost every continent on the planet. And believe me, we are more alike than we are different. Our relationship problems are very similar, and these principles 1 will be talking to you about in this book have been found effective across all cultures, demographics and sexual orientations. I will not be offering you "Pie in the Sky" and ungrounded information. And if anything I present is not clear or raises some questions for you, you will find my contact information at the end of this book and I would love for you to let me know so that I can serve you better.

From all my experience, I realize that much of the well-intended approaches we, including me, have used in the past to help couples in trouble and to help individuals find a soulmate, are misleading, if not harmful, or far too shallow to truly be effective to build unshakable passionate, joyful and secure loving. They are often remedies without a solid foundation to build upon, so they falter in the relationship moments of fear and misunderstanding.

In this book I am going to primarily share with you the most important foundational knowledge, along with some tips, that are vital to being able to have an amazing relationship with the person you are with currently, or that you hope to be with in the near future.

The incredibly powerful 5 practices I teach in my Deeper Soulmating Coaching Program are proven by scientific research and by many years of experience. They are called the "S-O-U-L-S Method." In the next section, I will explain more about these powerful 5. If you don't know these things, I can guarantee you that you will experience a great deal of unnecessary pain and confusion in relationships.

If you do know and practice these things, it will help you enormously in understanding what is actually going on in your relationship, and how to steer in the right direction to get to exactly what your heart desires. When you find yourself suddenly and surprisingly on a wrong and dangerous relationship argument/mis-understanding road, you will have a GPS to alert you and guide you back to a road that takes you and your co-passengers safely and joyfully to where you all really want to go.

And again, I want to emphasize the importance of the action of practice. Knowledge without action is impotent. You can supercharge your own relationship reality with positive, knowledgeable action!

My desire is to share with as many people around the globe as possible the depth and breadth of this life and relationship changing knowledge. For this purpose, I created the Deeper Soulmating Coaching Program, where individuals and couples can receive coaching and accountability and guided to in-depth successful practice of these simple but powerful principles in an invaluable supportive community family.

To get the very most out of this book now, I invite you to be in your highest and best self, allow yourself to be coachable, to be self honest, and be open to learning something new. Set judgment on the side for a moment to fairly allow yourself to fully experience a new point of view. These are the same attitudes that will allow you to be in a mutually empowering relationship with your beloved.

I see all relationships as potential diamonds, with many facets representing all the beautiful individual uniqueness and the potential connection points in the relationship. The beautiful brilliance of a diamond depends on the clarity of acceptance of each of those facets.

Throughout the book, I will be offering you some diamond facet clearing action tips. Please actively practice these tips to give yourself the amazing, brilliant and passionate relationship that you otherwise can only dream about.

So let's begin.

"To know thyself is the beginning of wisdom." — Socrates

Knowing WHAT, WHO, WHY and HOW, You Are. The answers that determine your experience of life.

WHAT ARE YOU?

Whether you are building a house, a business or building a love relationship, the number one principle is: you start from the ground up, Foundation First, if you want it to stand and be sustainable to the many natural challenges that will come. Here is a question that every human being needs to know the answer to, and yet it is never asked in the standard marriage\ therapy, couples counseling, relationship coaching or even in a find your soulmate coaching session. Most of us have never even thought about this question during our entire lifetime. And yet, your answer will determine your life and relationship experience.

The number one question is: *What* Am I?

If you don't know what something is, including yourself, you're going to make a lot of decisions about it and try to do a lot of things with it that are not going to be effective or successful and are going to lead to a lot of confusion and frustration. This is the fundamental question of all great spiritual traditions and all deep growth and personal transformational processes. This is about knowing your,"I am." There are a couple of ways of accessing an answer to this question, at least a knowing that is as deep as we can know anything as human beings. I was first exposed consciously to this question many decades ago by my healing meditation and transformational teacher, who led a small group of us in a process called Trespaso.

In the Trespaso experience, you sit across and knee to knee with a partner and either look into their eyes, or in some cases, into each other's third eye. One partner with caring, and without judgment, simply asks the other partner over, and over "what are you?" In some trainings, the question is "who are you" but that is not as deep a question, and we will talk more about the who later. I recommend you try this on your own with a mirror, or with your partner. With each answer to the question, the question automatically goes deeper. At first the answers start with "I am a human being", then deepen to "I am a man or woman", to "I am a leader, attorney, psychologist, mechanic, janitor, Etc", to "I am a mother, father, sister, brother, conservative, liberal, teacher, student, sick, healthy, angry, happy, a human body, a mind, etc, etc". Each time we answer the question, we peel away the onion and go deeper and deeper to our essential core.

For most who do this process with an open mind, as all these other identities fall away, there's a sense of something that is beyond all these names, and something about "I am" that has a sense of timelessness and not being attached to all these names and ideas or even attached to our physical body. I have experienced this with individuals from all parts of the world. Eventually, most come to "I am awareness", or "I am presence", or "I am spirit." On deeper discussion, most agree that these are words formed by our human verbal limitation to describe something that is the same thing, that is nothing.

For simplicity's sake, in this book, I will refer to all of these by using the word "spirit". "I am spirit". Most who come to this awareness also describe their sense of spirit as not being bounded by the body, and actually connected to or part of a boundless spiritual energy that is in everyone and everything. We are all connected.

Most people who consciously do this peeling away the onion exercise, describe the state that they go into as very similar to meditation or a deep prayerful state. They also describe that when they are experiencing themselves as spirit, there is a sense of needing nothing more, from anyone or anything. Presence is all there is, and in presence is the unlimited fertile void. Being has no neediness. Just imagine how that awareness alone could reduce emotional reactivity in your relationships.

There is another way that you can access a personal experience to answer the question of "what am I"? One advantage I have by being in the fourth quarter of my life game, is that while I have the sense that I will live quite a few years more, I know that I'm unlikely to live as many years in the future as I have lived in the past. That means I'm much closer than most to be able to meaningfully look over the edge and ask the question, "once I am finished with this amazing body, or it is finished with me, where will this consciousness that I identify as me, then be? "Another interesting question to ask open-mindedly is "where was I before I came into this body at birth?"

It is so vital that you know that you are, underneath it all, spirit, and believe it or not, so is your partner!

When you know that, what is actually going on in your relationship, in the moment, takes on a whole different perspective. We begin to see that all the other drama and suffering in our relationships is coming from somewhere else, from a much shallower place than the true depth of our connection. It is much easier to let go of petty differences, to forgive, and to give from this greater perspective. Once we truly see our partner or our prospective partner as spirit, we can never see them otherwise. All we need to do is to simply let ourselves simply *be present* with them.

Actually, if any of you have a hard time with the word spirit, and are put off or threatened by it, you don't really have to even think of it as spirit. All that is needed is to recognize that some energy comes into an individual's body when it is born, and at some point, it leaves that body. All you need to do is to be able to consider that energy is precious, and to treat it as though you feel it is precious.

When we get into the ridiculous fights that we all get into, and we become lost in the fog of war, all we have to do is take a breath and ask, what am I? What is he / she? Can you begin to see already how much more quickly we can get back on course to loving each other, when we really accept this deeper knowledge of What We Are? Just that knowledge, and acting upon it, changes everything!

DIAMOND FACET PRACTICE NUMBER ONE:

Do you want a huge, wonderful change in your relationship? Simply practice every morning when you wake up, asking the question and answering: What am I? What is he / she? Do it from your heart and Deep Mind. You will be amazed at how this changes your day. It seems too simple to be worthwhile, yet the simplest of contains the most powerful energy for change.

Consider the tiny atom, and it's incredibly useful or destructive power. Being present with WHAT you, your spouse and your kids are is just as powerful and creative. Lacking that awareness in any moment can also be massively destructive, in ways that even enter our genetic lineage.

Knowing the WHO, WHY and HOW of our identity are also incredibly necessary to know and be present to in our relationships and in our lives. This knowledge and the practices I will teach you, that are in alignment with this wisdom, will help you manage and avoid the challenges that naturally and purposefully come up in all relationships of significance. In my upcoming book, I will go into much greater detail of the science and art of knowing your answers to these questions also, along with how to be aligned with these for yourself and those you love, so you co-create extraordinary love, passion and joy with your spouse and for your children. We are talking about unshakable relationships on a foundation of soul.

So far, we have spoken only of the foundational principles, the "S" of the "SOUL METHOD." The "S" stands for Self Identity. Our deep answer to What, Who, Why and How we are. And being present to know the answers to these for our soulmate, spouse or partner and children. The "O" stands for Operating System (our brain in love). The "U" stands for Underlying State, Managing our energetic state to have peak connection. The "L" stands for Landmines , the emotional trigger states, and how to disarm and heal the painful and explosively destructive subconscious mines. The final "S' stands for Sexual Energetics, the passionate connection dynamics of the yin and yang of wonderful sexual energy.

Space in this book chapter does not allow further discussion of these here, but I can't wait to share all of this in my upcoming book and coaching program.

Thank you for your time and attention. Your unique soul and life really matter to all of us. Please speak your unique truth with kindness.

With blessings and gratitude, Dr. Allen

Scan or click on the above QR code to claim your bonus gifts and free resources from the featured authors! qrco.de/bcrTuK

Chapter 16

Narelle Shamrock

Imagine stepping into a time machine and traveling back to the 1990s. It was a time where the business environment was dynamic, there was a lot happening with opportunities for individuals at all levels as society went through one of its most intense changes.

This was a time of dynamic shifts in society and in business. The timeline shifted, and the known and the unknown became intermingled. There were political shifts, as Nelson Mandela re-entered society after a lifetime of incarceration. He became a political and transformational leader as he led an entire country through a chaotic time of impending chaos.

So much has changed. These were the years when people smoked on airplanes, in offices, in restaurants, in hotels, and in all parts of society. To call someone, you would call the person on their fixed landline. If they were not there, you would call again; patience and persistence were a part of life. If you were an early adopter, your mobile phone was the size and weight of a brick. Although, they started to reduce in size in a very short amount of time. Going from being a device which received and made calls to being a portable personal device.

The world started to speed up as the computer made its appearance in businesses and slowly into our homes. Imagine a world where there were no computers in homes! Today most of us have a mobile phone which has more capacity than the early computers. Google made its appearance on the scene in the late 1990s and slowly grew to be the go-to place to find information on pretty much everything. We went from having to know what we needed to know, going to the library at a university... to having access to pretty much anything we want in moments.

It was a time of significant change and the world we are in today was molded and changed into the life we are in today; it was a dance of evolving and adapting as each event would show up. Life sped up with more and more pressure to succeed and perform at a higher and higher level, regardless of our age.

Many of the changes that were happening were at a speed that enhanced growth but were happening at a speed wobble pace. Intermingled in all of the outward changes were catastrophic events which triggered off a series of crisis. Out of these crises were opportunities and growth.

In summary, in 30 years, the world has changed globally, almost without recognition. It has been a journey in evolving through challenges that have brought opportunities. It has been like being on an intricate roller coaster filled with highs and lows, often feeling like we are not in control.

So many of us have felt we have been controlled and manipulated by the chaos and crises that happen, many of us have found that life becomes a process of trying to paddle upstream instead of going with the flow and allowing ourselves to live our own and very best life.

If you are reading this, regardless of your age, you have been impacted directly or indirectly through your families by these changes. You need to congratulate yourself for getting through this time!

Let's travel back to today, back into your life.

We have seen how the past years have impacted every one of us and our focus has been on creating a predictable lifestyle. Our next step is to go through a few reflective questions to see exactly where you are on your journey.

Before we do this, meet Jenny. She is a young lady working in an office. She had worked for a few years in hospitality before joining a corporate working in an office. She had been in her job for a while and despite being promoted internally, getting recognition, and transferring between departments, she had started to find that she had reached a plateau and was not moving forward.

Your turn: When you look around you ...

- What does your life look like?
- Are you spending each day loving what you do?
- Are your relationships fulfilling and enhancing in your life?
- Are you rewarded financially for the daily effort you
  put in?

Stop a moment, take a breath, and write down what you are creating.

Let's find out how Jenny went when she took the time to really focus on doing this exercise. During our coaching conversations, when Jenny went through these questions, she realized that what she was creating was the opposite of what she wanted in her work life. She was experiencing bullying in the workplace. She was bypassed for promotions and was being given jobs that more junior staff were meant to do. Her work days were filled with a lot of frustration and conflict, and she was experiencing many things that she did not want. To make things even worse, it seemed like every time she was ready to make a change, something external or in her personal life would become chaotic. She would stop moving forward and try to protect herself from any more chaos. It was like she was repeating the things she did not want to create in her life.

This exercise of stopping and reviewing allowed her to see what was predictable in her life, even if it was not the outcome she was looking for.

Your Turn:

Take a moment and work through the areas of your life that you can see that are predictable.

Once you have established these areas, ask yourself: now that you have identified the areas of predictability, do you want more of ... or less of this type of predictable?

Wow, well done for taking these moments and reflecting on yourself!

You are now moving into the next stage of understanding more about yourself. You spend all day with yourself and yet, like most people, rarely spend the time getting to know what you truly want to achieve and what sort of life you want to live. We are either super busy running towards or away from life, being kept busy by social, home life, or exercise activities. We rarely ask ourselves what we want more of, and what we want less of.

Jenny went through this exercise, and she was super clear that she wanted less frustration, less conflict and more recognition for things she was doing well and achieving. Understanding what she truly wanted was an insight that she was able to blend into her vision for her career. She was able to create a picture, a visual of what she wanted. She also realized that adapting to all the changes in society and adapting to the advancement in technology is here to stay. She could not allow this to stop her from taking control of her life. She also recognized that she could not wait for something to catch up with her vision for herself. It is up to her to take control and consciously choose what she wants to show up in her life.

Your Turn:

Take a moment and identify what you want more of, and what you want less of in your life.

What are you consciously choosing in your life?

What do you want to see show up?

This is the vision of what you are wanting to create in your life.

Remember... by inviting in things you are choosing, you will need to show up, put yourself in the right places, do the studies or activities who make you the person that is the right person for this opportunity.

I invite you to consider this scenario: if you are wanting to do a 65 km walk over 3 days, there are very few of us that would have the stamina to take this on without some training, building up knowledge and strength in our bodies, getting the right equipment, hiking boots, etc, and investigating what will best support you. You would speak to other people who have done the same walk or a similar walk and would get their guidance. You would spend time with like-minded people who are supporting you, create a plan that is both achievable and will stretch you to make this a transformational experience.

I did a walk like this just over a year ago. I made sure that after I decided to do the walk; I was making sure that my feet were tough enough to do the distance and the hours, as the terrain was quite steep. The actual walk was much tougher than I could have imagined in intensity and so much more amazing than I could have expected in terms of an experience of being out in nature and exploring such a special part of our world, meeting people who were overcoming and breaking through their own personal paradigms.

It was the same for Jenny. Once she had decided what she wanted to create more of, she looked at the actual job she was doing, the environment, and her skills. She spent time really appreciating the value she brought to her team and the organization. Once she had done this, she realized that she was not aligned with the organization's values, and she decided on a career path that was more in alignment with her personal vision. Once she was clear on this, she looked at businesses looking for valuable team members to join their team and she chose the organization that would value her contribution, one she wanted to join and grow in.

Your Turn:

What activities, studies, conversations, up-skilling, knowledge and support do you need to create the life you are committed to living?

What are your skills and qualities that you bring to each experience?

Having a vision is incredibly powerful. W are often challenged by the lack of believing we deserve what we truly desire. Things from our past will often get in our way, the stories we tell ourselves, the conversations we have with ourselves. It *is* time to let go of the disempowering stories, and to start telling ourselves the empowering stories where we liberate our imagination and our inner strength by giving birth to a new story, our story.

Jenny found that once she had committed to a compelling vision where she was aligned and excited by what was happening, she started to change the way she viewed herself. The quality of the conversation with Jenny changed. She looked at the solution rather than the problems. She looked for opportunities and ways to improve each situation. By being more compassionate towards herself and those around her, she started to live the vision she was creating on a daily basis.

Your Turn:

What story are you telling yourself?

How are you choosing to change the quality of the conversation/story that you are having?

How can you be kinder and more compassionate with yourself?

It is time to take back your power and be resilient. You are making choices and creating a more compelling future where there is alignment with both your head and your heart by changing your story, by being kinder and more compassionate with yourself.

To summarize, you have taken these simple steps: taken the time to stop and evaluate, make choices that are yours, taken back control and treated yourself with compassion. You are now on the journey to create a more compelling present and future path.

When we first stepped into the time machine and stepped back 30 years, we saw that so much had happened in our lives and those we love. We were able to recognize that our next step was to ask ourselves what we truly wanted, or if we were going to allow ourselves to be controlled by those experiences and continue to live in the past.

By taking this journey, you have given yourself the gift of creating a compelling future, one that you are committed to and aligned with. Congratulations on giving yourself this gift.

Thrive and Prosper

Scan or click on the above QR code to claim your bonus gifts and free resources from the featured authors! qrco.de/bcrTuK

Chapter 17

Thank You For Reading Thrive & Prosper!

**Please Take Moment To Leave An
Honest Review On Amazon**

The authors have put a lot of love, attention, and care into this project!
We all would love your feedback and hearing what you have to say!

Please leave an honest **review on Amazon,** letting us know what
you thought of the book and how these stories and strategies have
impacted you.

We need your input to make the next version and future books even
better than this one.

Please head on over to **Amazon** and share your thoughts with us!

Thank you,

Mary Silver MSW and all Co-Author

Would You Like To Write Your Own Book?

Did you know Mary has been in the online coaching industry for over 14 years helping thousands of clients create success, become profitable, attract soulmate clients, and get their message out in BIG ways by writing a book?

She is an international best-selling author of the book, *Impact Millions - The Easiest Way to Attract Soulmate Clients Every Day!* She helps coaches and visionaries take their soul work, create a framework, write a book, get it published, market and sell the book so that it is monetized and brings in money year after year, while only working with soulmate clients, and doing purpose work that feeds the soul!

With Mary's unique system, she and her team help you:

- Craft your powerful message
- Create your unique framework that attracts your soulmate clients
- Build aligned profits paths
- Create your online dynasty
- Manifesting a wildly successful business that is centered on your soul work!

When you work with Mary and her team, you can expect to experience:

- The most streamlined and powerful way to build instant authority
- Be seen as the go-to expert in your field
- Have a beautifully finished, published book
- Attract your soulmate clients on autopilot
- A proven way to monetize your book so that it works for you day after day!

We invite you to discover how to write, publish, monetize, attract soulmate clients in day after day, while doing only your purpose work in as little as 90 days, so that you make more money, have more freedom, and live your best life!

Simply scan the picture below and claim your complimentary gift from us! *Become The Authority With Your Best Selling Book FAST - Workbook.* Let's create your lasting legacy today! qrco.de/bctqiy

Simply scan or click the QR code and lets create your lasting legacy today! qrco.de/bctqiy

About the Author

Mary Silver MSW is the international best-selling author of *Impact Millions - The Easiest Way to Attract Soulmate Clients Every Day*, who helps online coaches, inspiring authors, and visionaries get their message out in a BIG way by writing a book, so they can Impact Millions, work with their soulmate clients, while making the money they desire, doing their purpose work.

She has coached and mentored thousands of entrepreneurs helping them created an aligned business, attract more soulmate clients, and more profits, doing their purpose work. She believes and knows first hand the power of a book and the impact it can have by getting it published, and creating profit paths that lead to creating an online dynasty!

She is a master of mindset and helping her clients take the action needed through intuition and proven strategies to create a business they love. She received her Master's degree in Social Work in 1997, became a certified Law of Attraction Coach in 2009, holds numerous other certifications such as a Rapid Results Coach, Business Breakthrough Coach, Cash Injection Certified Coach and has spent over 20 in the professional field of helping people get what they want.

She is passionate about helping women gain financial independence and freedom by building an online business that is fueled by their passions! Her work includes helping her clients write and publish their books, create online courses, and create services that draw in their soulmate clients. She helps them with money mindset, so they quickly become profitable, business strategies, and guiding her clients to discover the way they love to run their business.

She has been seen on ABC, NBC, CBS, Fox, ASK, Thrive Global, Bustle, Medium, and many other media outlets. *Yahoo Finance recently interviewed her to showcase her work as one of the top 10 coaches to watch in 2021.* She is an award-winning coach named one of the top professionals in her field in 2018. For more information about Mary, visit www.marybaileysilver.com

facebook.com/TheMarySilver

twitter.com/TheMarySilver

instagram.com/marybaileysilver

Also by Mary Silver MSW

Impact Millions - The Easiest Way to Attract Soulmate Clients Every Day!

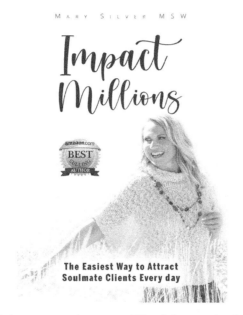

Click the picture to grab your copy of **Mary's International Best-Selling Book Impact Millions The Easiest Way To Attack Soulmate Clients Every Day!** *https://amzn.to/3qKMOlT*

Acknowledgments

I would like to share my heart-felt gratitude for all the people that helped create this book. I am so grateful for you! Thank you!

First, I'd like to thank my two coaches for all their encouragement and feedback on this project. Lise and Pagen, thank you so much for your edits and feedback. Also, thanks for holding the space for me to complete it quickly and with ease.

Next, I would like to thank my husband for his patience, and support throughout this project. Your love and support means the world to me. Thank you, babe! I love you!

Most of all, I would like to thank the authors that helped put this book together. Your attention to details, deadlines, and support have been so amazing. Thank you from the bottom of my heart! You are all fabulous!

Made in the USA
Las Vegas, NV
14 April 2022

47444109R10077